AF348526

A Guest Again

Peter Siedzick

ISBN 0-7414-3273-0

Published by:

INFI⚲ITY
PUBLISHING.COM

1094 New DeHaven Street, Suite 100
West Conshohocken, PA 19428-2713
Info@buybooksontheweb.com
www.buybooksontheweb.com
Toll-free (877) BUY BOOK
Local Phone (610) 941-9999
Fax (610) 941-9959

Printed in the United States of America

Printed on Recycled Paper

Published August 2006

INTRODUCTION

This book started out as a travelogue, more or less. When my beloved wife, Susan, passed away in the summer of 2004, after all too brief a marriage, I was living in Bandon, a wonderful little village on the south Oregon coast that becomes a bit inhospitable during the winter rains. I resolved to temporarily leave the town that winter and, I hoped, some of the sad memories of her two year long ordeal, and distract myself with a trip to see the rest of the United States and some of my friends and family.

In the course of deciding where to go and who to see, I made the effort to contact some long-lost high school and college classmates, most of whom I hadn't seen for decades. In every case I was greeted with enthusiasm, warmth and promises of hospitality. I plotted a path that would take me around the country, seldom having to stay in hotels for more than two nights in a row, and began to think of the trip as my Great American Cross Country Freeload.

On other journeys, before my marriage, I had carried a tape recorder and made notes about places I was seeing for the first time, or about my life's situation, then transcribed the notes into narratives for my friends. I still had a mini-cassette recorder and a lot of tapes from those days, and I also carried a notebook computer for transcriptions. This work is the result.

Along the way, I found my attitudes shifting. Raised an Easterner I wanted to return to the places in the East that had always seemed so attractive to me, but I found that what made them attractive was the people I knew who lived in them. Sometimes tired of looking at the wide-open spaces of the West, I discovered that I longed for them after too many miles of heavily treed Eastern highways.

Most of all, I discovered that I could not outrun my grief, nor the sad memories of my wife. I had to learn to sort out the good memories from the horrible ones of her final days. And I had to learn to live with all of them. At home.

Thanks to Bob and Mary Ellen for continued encouragement along the way, and to Linda, my editor, who gave me focus.

Peter Siedzick
Bandon, Oregon, 2006

PART ONE
FROM SEA TO SHINING SEA

RENO

The pre-dawn hush of Bandon-by-the-Sea is a tonic to those of us who have lived the majority of our lives in the bustling big cities. On the morning of my departure there was no one stirring, there were no car headlights to blind me, and no illuminated windows except the one dimly casting its 100 watts from the lighthouse tower across the Coquille River. Quiet, still and dark, Bandon slept as I set out on my Great Adventure.

I really was thinking of the trip as My Great Escape. While Bandon had been the site of my most intimate moments with my beloved wife, Susan, it had also been the place where the horrors of her final, wasting days had occurred. I sought release from the latest memories and knew I needed time to get over them, time to learn to focus on the happier moments we had spent together. I believed it would be easier to do that in different surroundings.

I'd kept busy planning for the trip for several months. I'd written numerous lists, and packed and checked and re-checked, but for the first half-hour of the journey a thought plagued me that I had forgotten something, I'd forgotten something. At about the time I crossed the river in the town of Coquille it occurred to me: I'd taken no water. "Well," I thought, "I can fix that in Myrtle Point", and so, ten or so miles further down the road I stopped at one of the town's markets for a six-pack.

Ever walk into a room and get the feeling that you're dressed improperly, as if everyone is formal and you're

casual? I felt that way in the market because all the custom-
ers were wearing cammies - camouflage clothing to the
uninitiated. Even a husband and wife were in his-and-hers
cammies. It was October 28th, it may have been the start of
hunting season, or perhaps the locals wear cammies to hide
from the salmon when they go fishing. Fish were in the
rivers, after all, awaiting the winter rains that would swell
the streams and allow them to run to their spawning beds. In
any case, I felt a little out of it, bought my water and slunk
from the store, trying to be invisible in jeans and windbreaker.

And drove on to Remote, OR. That name conjures
up images of a tiny hamlet of hardy and self-sufficient souls,
hidden in the rugged fastnesses of Oregon. Alas, not so. It
lives on a looping road that intersects OR 42 at points about
¾ of a mile apart and consists of a general store and several
houses. Not so remote, not so unusual, and it doesn't live up
to its intriguing name, but someone's heart was in the right
place. I didn't notice if there was a post office, but what
would you think about getting mail postmarked "Remote"?
Had it been packed out by mule?

The route east from the sea ascends the coastal range
of the Northwest, the mountain chain that, though not very
high, blocks the clouds and causes the winter rains to soak
the coastal plains. After climbing it for about a thousand
feet, I leveled off at Camas Valley.

Camas is an edible root, or at least I believe it is after
I read about the Lewis and Clark expedition. Hungry after
traversing the Bitterroot Mountains, and lacking any game to
kill and eat, the Corps of Discovery was fortunate to find
friendly Indians who gave them the camas root to eat.
Camas Valley must have had, at one time or another, an
abundance of the plant, hence its name, but I haven't a clue
as to what camas looks like, and I can't say if it's still there.

In town there are a few interesting road names.
There's a Hard Cash Lane, for example, and outside of town

there's a Boy Scout camp located on Suicide Creek Lane. Imagine the campfire stories at that place.

When it comes to lanes, though, I think Bandon takes the prize. We have, a few miles to the south of town and off US 101, a road called Lois Lane, but I've no idea if it was named with Clark Kent's heartthrob in mind. That reminds me that Margot Lane, "companion" to Lamont Cranston, The Shadow, was allegedly a cousin to Lois. Betcha didn't know that. By the way, did the word "companion" connote in the 1930s the same thing that "significant other" does today?

The last landmark before reaching Interstate 5 was the Roseburg Lumber mill in Dillard. I passed it too early for the day shift to put the plant into full swing, but it appeared as though it was busy, nevertheless. The Dillard plant produces pressed fiberboard for the most part, and some milled lumber and plywood, but it is, like the rest of the Northwest lumber industry, a shadow of its former self.

I-5 in southern Oregon is a virtual roller coaster, cutting across valleys and climbing to nearly 2,000 feet in several instances. At one of the crests I passed the smoking remains of someone's camper trailer. The fire could not have happened more than a few hours before, but the fire trucks were gone and several people still stood in the mist, looking disconsolate, their shattered dreams smoldering by the road. I felt their loss and my helplessness and continued on.

There are several place names on I-5 that just beg investigation. Jumpoff Joe Creek. Indian Mary Park. I tried to research these places on the Internet later and met with limited success. Jumpoff Joe Creek was named after Joe McLoughlin, member of a trapping party camped on the stream in 1828, who came into camp after dark, fell off the edge of the bluff and received some serious injuries. His unsympathetic comrades stuck him, and the creek, with the nickname "Jumpoff". It sounds like "the guys" haven't changed much since 1828.

A related internet hit revealed that, exactly one hundred fifty years later, in 1978, a Southern California man, living on his family's ¾ acre site in a trailer near the creek, heard stomping sounds outside and concluded that he was visited by a sasquatch, or Bigfoot. He should have invited it in to share whatever he was smoking, but there's no record in his Internet testimonial that he did.

Indian Mary Park, obviously named after someone called Indian Mary, is the smallest Indian reservation in the country, but that's all I could find out. I still don't know who Indian Mary was, nor do I even know her tribe. There has to be an explanation at the park, but I have never stopped.

At the city of Rogue River, there is a sign indicating the Savage Rapids Dam. There's another side trip for exploration, but I'll bet the dammed water has submerged the savage rapids.

I had thought to continue on I-5 south to Mt. Shasta, CA where a state highway could take me to Susanville, but when I pulled off near Ashland to study the map, I found that I could take OR 66 over to Klamath Falls. Then I could continue to Alturas and down the eastern slope of the Sierra Nevada to Reno, my destination for the day. It seemed that this route would avoid some of the snow in the Sierra that had been reported on TV, so I decided to take it. I would also miss the highest point on I-5, Siskiyou Summit, where the road climbs steeply to over 4,000 feet, not a route for me to traverse in winter conditions.

Off OR 66 there's a road called Dead Indian Memorial Road. But, wait a minute, aren't "Dead" and "Memorial" more or less the same thing? That reminded me of Live Oak Avenue in Arcadia, California. Would we name a street Dead Oak Avenue? Somewhere, on one of those Word of

The Day things, I was introduced to "pleonasm", meaning the usage of more words than necessary to describe something. Judging by the media, and the entertainment industry, pleonasm is rampant in the United States, and I'm not just referring to the filler phrase, "like, you know". Of course pleonasm has always been alive and well in American politics.

Route 66, not to be confused with US 66 farther south, promised to be scenic and interesting as it wound upwards from the valley containing Ashland to cross the lower Cascades. All too soon, however, I was stopped for a construction project and then became the fourth vehicle in a small convoy. This curse proved a blessing, though, as we clomb ever higher into clouds and fog, and the twists and turns proved torturous, slowing us down to 25 mph. I could not see beyond two cars in front of me, and although aware of a steep drop off to my right, the view was obscured by the clouds. Good for my fear of heights.

Eventually, the other cars turned off, the fog dissipated, and I reached level ground of thick pine forest. I began to enjoy a pretty drive with varying shades of green in the different conifers. At one point I saw a brown creature feeding in the woods and my first reaction was that it was a horse, but I never did see the critter's head. Since there were no fences to keep domestic animals from the highway, I concluded that it must have been an elk. A big elk.

After the climb and construction and convoy, the road now ran on the straight and level through a corridor of pines. In the meantime, snow had appeared under and in the trees and the overall effect was idyllic. I passed the summit of Hayden Mountain, 4,695 feet, even higher, but not steeper than Siskiyou Pass on the Interstate, and started downward towards the Klamath Valley, spotting a sign that said, "Live Stock". "Here we go again," I thought, "Would we be concerned about Dead Stock?"

As I entered the Klamath River's floodplain, the sun came out, the sky turned blue from its leaden gray and I drove through pastoral ranch country. The road detoured around Klamath Falls, where I spent an entire week one night, and I picked up OR 39, heading for California.

On a previous trip through the area, I had seen protest signs by the farmers/ranchers about Klamath River water. According to the locals, Klamath Lake's level was being held high to facilitate procreation of some suckerfish. No signs were in evidence this trip, though, and fields appeared to be pretty green, so the problem must have been resolved.

As I understand it, the farmers were blaming the conservationists for retaining water for a useless fish. Later, when salmon died in the Lower Klamath River for lack of water, the conservationists blamed it on the farmers. I take no sides. Well, yes I do. The conservationists don't want us to catch the salmon or cut trees, and they don't want the farmers to have enough water to raise crops. What are they going to eat if they have their way with us? I'm not a Sierra Club member, by the way.

I've called them farmers, but for a long distance I saw nothing but hayfields and pasturage, so perhaps they are rightly called ranchers. But outside of Merrill, CA I saw crops being harvested, they looked like onions or garlic, good high desert crops. Later a truck FULL of potatoes turned off the highway to enter a plant called Newell Potatoes. So farmers there are.

About fifteen miles into California the land began to change from cropland to desert, abundant with sagebrush and pinion pine. I passed through the California Agricultural Inspection Station and the bearded guy in his rumpled uniform tore himself away from looking out the window to actually ask me if I had any produce. He must have been bored in this out-of-the-way station and needed someone to talk to. Usually they just wave me through.

As I followed the straight road from Klamath Falls to Canby, CA the snow accumulation on the side of the road became deeper and the thick, wooly clouds lowered themselves to a nearly touchable ceiling. The sagebrush disappeared and the trees got taller and taller, a sure sign that I was climbing, however gently. A light wind blew snow from the branches of the pines and the effect brought to mind the song, "Winter Wonderland", but I quickly came back to reality as I remembered I still had a long drive and I didn't want road conditions to get worse.

At Canby I was driving through a large bowl surrounded by snow covered hills. Canby, population not much, elevation not high. A good place to drive *through*.

I was headed for Alturas, CA, for a number of reasons, first being that I had never been there; that's always a good reason for me to go someplace. Second, I would be driving about the same distance as if I had gone straight down the road to Susanville. And third, I believed that the road south from Alturas would be on the eastern slope of the Sierras and hence, snow free, as opposed to the road past Eagle Lake which I thought to be more likely snow-covered and dangerous.

And, oh yes, I once ran into some people from Alturas on the crabbing dock in Bandon and they described it as high desert, so I wanted to be able to tell them I'd been there if they ever showed up again.

Well, as it turned out, the only snow I actually drove through all day was on the streets of Alturas. County and/or State highway people had plowed whatever snow there was off of the road surfaces into and out of Alturas, but the city streets had been totally neglected and were full of rutted slush. The only nice thing was the pretty effect of snow on the still-green cottonwoods and willows in and around town.

In case you think I overly fear winter driving conditions, let me set the record straight. I was raised in Rhode

Island, lived in Rochester, New York and Denver, Colorado and know very well how to drive in snow and ice – not fast, and with as little braking as possible. None of my history, though, means that I should *want* to drive in that stuff.

South of Alturas I followed US 395, a very uninspiring road, through flat land with bare hills to either side. The only break in the monotony came in the town of Likely, CA, speed limit 40 mph, home of some of the biggest Angus bulls I've ever seen. There were the Likely Store and the Likely School and I'm sure some old timers in town can tell a Likely Story.

My lack of taped comments from this point on indicates that I was getting tired or bored, or both. I by-passed Susanville on a county road, missed the city limit sign where Susan had once posed for a picture, unable to stop grinning in front of "her town", and picked up US 395 again on the other side of a hairpin leg to press on for Reno. Snow had disappeared by the time I approached Susanville and I had a straight, dry run into Reno, the Circus Circus hotel and a good and inexpensive night's sleep. And so ended Day One of Peter Siedzick's Great American Cross Country Freeload.

SALT LAKE

Good Morning, Reno. Goodbye, Reno. I left the hotel before 8AM to fight the few short blocks of downtown city traffic to reach the Interstate. As much as I like to travel the back roads of America and see it firsthand, there aren't many ways of doing so in Nevada, or, for that matter, Utah and Wyoming. The one option in Nevada is US 50, nicknamed the Loneliest Road in America. I'd been there, done that, said, "Yes, it is," so Interstate 80 it was. Besides, as I was to remind myself throughout the first part of the trip, I had committed to being at my sister's house in Delaware for Thanksgiving, less than four weeks away. That, combined with a few other schedule constraints, was to dominate my thinking about route choice until then.

Despite being tired the evening before, I had decided to explore downtown Reno and test Lady Luck. I learned very little about the city on a cold, dark night and ended up about even on the video poker machines. It was still better than sitting in the room watching TV, I suppose.

There were about 400 miles to West Wendover, NV on the Utah state line, where I intended to spend the night in another inexpensive room. When I considered the distance I had to travel I was pleased to be in my big car, a Mercury Grand Marquis, MGM Grand, for short. It's a smooth-riding, comfortable car with a roomy interior and a large trunk that carried everything I might need on the long trip. It turned out that a lot of the stuff I took was excess, but the engineer in me thought, "Better safe than sorry." I never was a Boy Scout, so "Be Prepared" didn't enter my mind.

As I started out on I-80 I realized that I had never gone in this direction on this highway, so it was, for practical purposes, virgin road. And I like virgin road.

I-80 follows the Truckee River from Reno for about 30 miles. Originating at Lake Tahoe, the Truckee flows down from the Sierra, through Reno, and empties into Pyramid Lake. Pyramid Lake is on an Indian reservation, Paiute, as I recall. Once a fisherman's paradise, increasing demands for water by "civilization" have lowered the lake's level. The fishing isn't as good anymore, I hear.

Pyramid Lake was named by John Fremont. One of our lesser-hailed American heroes, Fremont was a brilliant cartographer who mapped much of the West. He was admired greatly by Kit Carson who guided him through many of his adventures. By the way, I read where Carson has been criticized for getting lost on at least one expedition. Think about it, how can you get lost in unexplored country? You ARE lost. My friend, Bob, says he's never been permanently lost, and it must be true, he's at home as I write.

Anyway, Fremont, a highly educated man, thought the rock protruding from the lake was similar to the Great Pyramid of Cheops, hence the name. Further south, as a gesture of mutual admiration, Fremont named the Carson River and the Carson Valley.

I once visited Pyramid Lake on a day with low overcast. The Indians had named a rock formation near the lake as the Earth Mother, the Place Where Everything Began. As I watched the sky descend into the lake and the misty lake ascend into the clouds that day, I understood why the Indians held the place in awe and reverence. I certainly did.

I didn't visit Pyramid Lake on this trip, though. Instead I followed the Truckee through its canyon, noting the cottonwoods varying their leaf shades from brilliant yellows through pale greens, all backlit by an early morning sun. I didn't remember this rather spectacular canyon from the one previous visit, when Susan and I were passing through in the other direction, with our sights set on reaching Lake Tahoe. It may have been one of those episodes when *she* was driving:

"Did you see that?" she asked.

"See what?"

"That remarkable tree over there," she replied, not indicating where "there" was.

"No, I was watching the road".

"Why were you doing that?"

"One of us has to".

Once out of the canyon of the Truckee, I flicked on cruise control, as this road was made for it, and I had had very few occasions to use it before. Actually, I never had used cruise control in Southern California; there was always too much traffic for it to make sense.

Crossing the Truckee as it swung north up to the Lake, I continued eastward past the exit for Fallon, NV and the Fallon Naval Air Station, home of the Top Gun school. I didn't see Tom Cruise or any other naval aviators, though. I did see some rather muddy "dry" lakebeds. Not easily navigable during the winter, those lakes.

When I passed mile marker 50, I remembered that most of the states I have been in put mile markers on their highways. On Interstate highways, exit numbers usually correspond to the nearest mile marker, all of which makes it easier for the driver to know where he is and how far it is to where he is going. In accordance with its policy of being The Other State, California does not have mile markers. I read that the state was going to install them, but they haven't, probably due to a recent budget crisis, which cost a governor his job. I don't know why they don't want to let their people know where they are; it seems to me that most Californians have an identity crisis as it is. Now at last, though, I was in a state with mile markers and I knew I had about 360 miles to Wendover. Even though miles are numbered from west to east, my Rand-McNally road map told me what my exit number was. Simple arithmetic let me calculate the distance left. Am I anal? Sure.

I've made several pointed remarks about California and Californians, and I'm bound to make more; it's not my favorite place. During the first few years of my marriage, I slowly came to understand that Susan, who had immigrated with her husband and children directly to Los Angeles in 1981, had visited very little of the rest of the United States. Consequently, her opinions of America had been formed by the attitudes and values of Southern California. I did my best, within our means, to explore with her the rest of America and show her that So Cal was the deviation, not the norm. Dominated by Hollywood and overrun with illegal immigrants of every stripe, the Southern California basin is NOT the typical American melting pot. It's more like a cauldron of different oils that refuse to mix.

An exit sign read, "Nightingale Hot Springs" and, sure enough, there were numerous plumes of steam rising from the ground. I tend to forget that there are lots of places in Nevada with geothermal activity. As I watched the steam, I was passed by a truck from the Platte Valley Express, headquartered somewhere in Nebraska. I supposed that he could follow I-80 all the way home. So much for the romantic life of a truck driver; to me, watching America from the Interstate is like watching grass grow.

I used to like the desert, and I can still see an element of beauty in it, but the starkness of rock and sand is in sharp contrast to the lush vegetation where I live now. I suppose I like the greenery better. The desert used to represent an escape to me; I could leave Los Angeles behind and fill the windshield with nothingness, avoid the asphalt and neon, the unreadable and garish Asian and Hispanic signs... Now the desert is just a place to cross.

Ahead of me I saw cottonwoods marking the path of the Humboldt River; behind me was the Humboldt Sink, where a flowing river just disappears into the ground. The Carson River has its own sink, and the trail between them, some 40 or 50 miles, was one of the hardest stretches for the 49ers, who followed the Humboldt downstream and the Carson upstream to the foot of the Sierras. I read that one can still find abandoned gear in that portion of desert.

In the Great Basin of America, which is mostly in Nevada, water flows in, none flows out. The Humboldt and Carson Rivers end in sinks; the Truckee and Walker fill lakes.

To relieve the monotony of the Interstate I decided to take the Business 80 sections through some of the cities of Nevada. In Lovelock, I saw rather neat buildings, the ubiquitous casino and a few Mexican restaurants. An old gent riding his three-wheeled power scooter gave me a friendly wave as I passed through. "Just like Bandon," I thought.

In Winnemuca, a thriving town, there was a Holiday Inn Express and a Red Lion, not exactly your mom and pop kind of places. Casinos were doing a heavy trade at 10AM, and there was a general air of prosperity. A sign on the Interstate said "Butch Cassidy Left Here Rich, So Can You." Winnemuca is not dying of Interstate Bypass Disease.

Several times, I had seen dead critters on the side of the road, usually pounded to a pulp, and wondered, "What kind of animal lives in the middle of the desert?" Now, outside of Winnemuca, I was able to identify one as a coyote. "Of course," he said, slamming his forehead with the heel of his hand. That one was near a sign for Pumpernickel Valley, an imaginative name in the desert.

On the Battle Mountain business loop I saw more liquor stores than anything else on the outskirts. Must be a thirsty town. There were a few dingy casinos, but really nothing to brag on at Battle Mountain. In fact, a billboard claimed "Battle Mountain, Voted The Armpit of America by

The Washington Post. Make Us Your Next Pit Stop." I love their sense of humor in Battle Mountain, but found little else to admire.

By contrast, Elko was booming. There were several large casinos, one of which now has nineteen of my dollars, but I also got lemon meringue pie and coffee for $2.66, so I ought not complain. Incidentally, the local radio station in Elko is KELK. Of course.

I once met a guy from Elko on the crabbing dock in Bandon; the only real-life person I'd ever met named Zane. He and his family had driven straight through and were catching their limits of crab to take back for a crab feast. I seem to recall that he said it was a fourteen-hour drive in his RV. Imagine, a neighborhood crab feast in the middle of the desert with fresh crab. I have since driven the route they took, from Winnemucca over to Klamath Falls. It rivals US 50 for loneliness.

The next highway sign said, "Frequent Deer Crossing". I've seen a "Major Deer Crossing" and even saw a major deer at it once, but I'd never seen a frequent deer. Still haven't.

I-80 follows river courses through Nevada in a generally east-west direction. Doing so takes the traveler around, rather than over, the numerous mountain ranges in the state. I once read that a relief map of Nevada looks like a bunch of caterpillars creeping southward, and I suppose it does. US 50 climbs some of those caterpillars, but today, on I-80, I avoided most of them.

Carlin, NV's billboard said, "Where The Trains Stop and The Gold Rush Begins". I'll bet that was a contest winner – sponsored by the Chamber of Commerce.

Wendover, UT and West Wendover, NV are, for all intent and purpose, the same town, clustered about old Wendover AFB. The base was the original training site of the Enola Gay, carrier of the American version of The Final

Solution to Hiroshima. The town has casinos and large hotels on the Nevada side and just a few motels and stores on the Utah side. I had been advised to visit the base, but missed the turnoff and had to be content with the sighting of several old hangers. Months later, on another trip to the East, I stopped at the base and visited its museum, complete with a replica of Little Boy signed by Col. Paul Tibbetts, among others.

Throughout this trip, I missed opportunities to explore side roads and see places of interest. When planning the trip, I had decided that seeing people was of more importance than visiting places and had scheduled myself to be with folks at certain times. This trip, at least, had to follow those constraints. The next trip will be to places.

After the sign for the Bonneville Speedway, I stopped at a rest area where a guy was actually mowing grass. The stretch of desert between Wendover and Salt Lake City is virtually one large dry lakebed. Why is there State-maintained grass in the middle of the desert?

When I reached Salt Lake City I followed Lew's directions through town and up the canyon on the east side to where he and Linda live in a magnificent home high above the city. And so began my first adventure as a guest, but not yet a guest again.

DENVER

Lew and I were classmates at West Point; more than that, we were friends who had endured the rigors of plebe year together and had a few adventures when we "escaped" The Point on Choir trips. Linda is a vivacious and captivating redhead, with a mischievous eye and a ready chuckle. She had come to New York from their native Pennsylvania for a number of dates with Lew and we had met well before Graduation and our respective marriages.

Lew has been very successful as the CEO of several companies he was hired to bring back to profitability. None of them, though, has yet reached the level of AOL, founded by a classmate of ours. And yet another classmate is chairman of the New York Stock Exchange, but I don't rub elbows with those guys.

It snowed while I was at Lew and Linda's home, miles up a canyon overlooking the city, but by Sunday afternoon the roads were clear enough for Lew to take me on a quick tour of Salt Lake City, Temple Square, and the university. In general we had a great time, just resting and relaxing and discussing new and old times. As the old saying goes, there really are no friends like old friends. Life's mundane pursuits seem to become insignificant when true old friends gather.

There are several ways to get from Salt Lake City to Denver, some passing spectacular views of the Rockies, but I chose to sacrifice aesthetics for time and took I-80. Besides, there was reported snow in the Rockies. I left on a perfectly clear day with beautiful sunshine; I-80 was clear and dry and I had to ascend from Salt Lake City for twenty-five miles or so before I saw any more snow. I thought, as I began to anticipate the drive through Wyoming, that I would be terribly bored on this leg of the trip, but that it might be for the last time until I hit Texas.

On an earlier trip in the other direction, Susan, my beloved English wife, born in the city of Manchester, had marveled at the limitless plains of Wyoming and the fact that we drove for over a hundred miles without sighting a tree. Here I realized with a great deal of sadness that on this trip I was looking at the world through only one pair of eyes, and that removed some of the grandeur.

Western Wyoming, home of Rock Springs and Green River, brings to mind only one word: badlands. What vegetation I saw was sparse and unhealthy looking, and I thought it an area best passed through quickly. I crossed the Continental Divide at 6,940 feet and thought it was now downhill to the other "shining sea".

But I reached the Continental Divide again at elevation 7,000 feet, and I was on a high, relatively level plateau. It was hard to believe that this was a point on the line dividing water flow to the Atlantic or the Pacific. I reflected that I wouldn't come back to "my" side of The Divide until I reached Arizona on the way back home. Later, I found out that it would actually be in New Mexico.

I expected to see some antelope herds along the route, but none appeared until I was quite close to Laramie, my exit point from I-80 and from Interstate highways in general, I hoped. I finally spotted a small herd of one buck and six or seven does about twenty miles outside of Laramie, and then, as I crossed open prairie with the Medicine Bow Range behind me there were more herds. It was good to know they're still around. Also around were cattle, prime Angus beef on the hoof, soon to appear on your supermarket shelves.

Years before, as I was moving my family west, I had read "Centennial", James Michener's wonderful and glorified book about Colorado. Soon thereafter, I found myself staying overnight in Laramie and, in search of a good steak, being directed to Centennial, Wyoming, at the edge of the Medicine Bow range. Three of us shared a steak almost too big for us and, though I've never re-visited Centennial, my memories of it are still warm. There is no Centennial, Colorado, unless they've named once since. Later, on a trip near Cheyenne, I saw a sign for The Old Corral Hotel and Steakhouse in Centennial. Has to be the same place. Cheyenne is also the home of Curt Gowdy State Park, and I remembered him as the voice of the Boston Red Sox, then of the AFL and finally, as the host of American Sportsman, back when hunters actually killed animals.

And once, on a trip from Casper down to Laramie, I looked forward to visiting the town of Medicine Bow, a truly colorful name from the Old West. Imagine my disappointment when, instead of boarded sidewalks, false fronts and a saloon, the town turned out to be four buildings and a gas station at a crossroads. Oh, well… Obviously, the wide-open and windswept prairies of Wyoming give rise to musing and more musing.

"Welcome", the sign said, "to Colorful Colorado". The temperature was twenty degrees, some welcome. I followed US 287 down to Fort Collins, passing through Laporte, CO, home of a cement plant where I used to make sales calls. The structure was still there though I think the cement operation ceased years ago, as had the company I used to work for. Passages, passages.

Fort Collins was established as a military post in 1864, during a time of severe troubles with local Indian tribes in Colorado. The area of the Cache La Poudre valley had become popular with settlers who had either given up searching for gold in the Rush of '59, or who had established businesses to support the miners who were still working.

Cache La Poudre, by the way, is a river named by French Canadian trappers who cached a large supply of their powder along its banks. Collins was Col. Collins, the commander of some Ohio troops at Fort Laramie, WY. And that's all I'm going to say about that, it's all I know.

I drove down North College Avenue, the main street of the town, during the rush hour and was surprised at the heavy traffic. The old town shopping area seemed quite nice, albeit filled with functional stores, not trendy or tourist shops. I was interested in a possible move to Fort Collins, to be closer, but not too close, to my grandchildren in Denver. I wanted to gather literature firsthand, so after a night's rest I visited the Chamber of Commerce for re-location information.

I had made sales calls in Fort Collins during the '70s and '80s when it was a much smaller town, so I knew my way around, and after circling Colorado State University, I took a remembered back route to Loveland. The trees were in color, the sun was shining and, at one point when I topped a rise after joining US 287, I could see the entire Front Range down to Pike's Peak. The Range was covered in snow and Long's Peak stuck up like a white pyramid. It was a magnificent sight and I felt drawn to the area, as I had been in 1975 when I forsook New York and moved to the West.

Berthoud, a small town south of Loveland, hadn't changed much in twenty years, but there were cars parked everywhere along the main street. It was Election Day, and I had voted long before, thanks to Oregon's mail-in balloting system, so I assumed that here, voters had parked wherever they could. That also brought to mind that I had seen a lot of Kerry/Edwards signs in Fort Collins and Loveland, but virtually no Bush/Cheney signs. I had listened to the analysts on TV that morning and concluded that nobody really KNEW how the election was going to go. I wondered how many people like me were going to ready the ballot, look at it and think, "Better the devil you know…" Judging from the results, a lot.

A bumper sticker on the car in front of me said, "Lick Bush in '04". Speaks for itself. Later on I saw another car with a Kerry bumper sticker on one side, "I Brake For Prairie Dogs" on the other. That speaks for itself, too.

I drove through Longmont and Boulder. I lived in Boulder for a year after my divorce in the early 80s, but I had never quite gotten used to the town. This day I fought traffic on the Boulder Turnpike that was quite heavy despite it being early afternoon and finally got to a hotel in Aurora.

Dinner that night was with my daughter, Stephanie. Steph was fighting breast cancer and undergoing chemotherapy prior to surgery. She had been hospitalized when her white cell count went too low, so next day, I sat with her during her doctor's consultation, wanting to know what his care plan was. I had had to learn about chemotherapy during Susan's ordeal, and understood that Steph's first treatment had been too harsh. It seemed to me that the doctor had a handle on the remainder of the treatment process, but when it came time to accompany Steph into the treatment room I balked and excused myself. I simply could not endure the sight of so many cancer patients; it was too soon after my loss of Susan. Today, a year later, after chemo shrank her tumor, and Stephanie had surgery and radiation she is cancer–free.

Stephanie is my middle child and was the most difficult, yet most loving of my children. She'd gone through a really rotten divorce and still showed some bitterness, but her courage and determination through the cancer event stirred some feelings of parental pride. She is a survivor.

Next day, I had lunch with Mary Ellen on what turned out to be her birthday. She is still one of the most beautiful women I know. We lunched in a trendy spot in the Cherry Creek area of Denver, and she was reluctant to let me know it was her birthday, knowing that I'd want to pick up the check and not wanting to appear mercenary. I did pick up the check and will never think of Mary Ellen as mercenary.

Mary Ellen and I had dated in the 80s, while between our respective marriages, and collaborated on a book effort, "Real Texans Don't Brag". Don't look for it at your local bookstore. I still have the manuscript, but have long since destroyed the rejections.

Lunch the next day was with Ken and Shirley. Ken was a former boss and mentor, and we met at the Fresh Fish Company, a restaurant I remembered from my years in Denver. It is next door to The Proof of The Pudding, a one-time meat market where I was highly unsuccessful in my single years. Ah, the memories!

My son, Mike, was nearing the end of a two-year call-up in the Army Reserve. His unit, a training command, had been assisting combat units to prepare for deployment to Afghanistan and Iraq. I was anxious to see him and learn if I had finally gotten smart. You see, my own father didn't really get smart until I turned 30, so I had looked forward to the day when Mike reached his 30th, only to discover that I was no smarter than before. When I recalled that my father had been much older at my birth than I'd been at Mike's, and that he had actually become smart at 64, I began to look forward to that age, and now that I'd reached it, wanted Mike to confirm that I was, at last, making sense.

But in one of life's disappointments, Mike was down in Texas instead of at Fort Carson, CO, and I would have to wait until Christmas to see him. I visited with my delightful daughter-in-law, Laura, a noble woman who has held the fort, her job, her children, a new house, and God knows what else during my son's absence, and with my equally delightful grandsons. Then I returned to Fort Collins for a day of real estate lessons.

There was a time when I looked at retiring to an iso-
lated place with acreage, and I could still have that kind of
isolation in the Cozy Coastal Cottage of Coos County.
Without Susan, though, I didn't think I could bear it, I felt
that I would need to be with more people. After my divorce
I had had to learn to cope with being alone, of no longer
being half of a whole; now, I had to learn to do it again. I
believed that Fort Collins, with a larger population, a
university with attendant cultural attractions and a pretty
moderate climate could fill the bill.

I looked at a number of new home developments and
a number of female realtors. One location and house plan
was particularly attractive and so was the lady flogging it. I
resolved then and there, however, not to let my decision be
influenced by an attractive and large-breasted blonde realtor.
And, so far, it hasn't.

GRAND ISLAND

When I finished with my tour of Fort Collins I left Mike and Laura's house and headed east to Nebraska. I felt that I had had my fill of Interstate highways and resolved, when and where possible, to avoid them for the remainder of the trip, to drive through rural America emulating William Least Heat Moon on his "Blue Highways".

I drove east on CO 52 to Fort Lupton, where, in 1836, a Lieutenant Lancaster Lupton liked what he saw there and settled, only to leave in 1844 after droughts and storms changed his mind. Fort Lupton was re-settled during the Colorado gold rush of 1859 and is now a pleasant farming community, where kids actually carry their books to school. Southern California kids seem to need wheeled suitcases.

The country east of Fort Lupton is rolling terrain, gently sloped country with lots of agriculture, sheep but no cattle, chicken farms; it's Heartland country. At Hudson, CO, I was at first surprised to see a Mexican restaurant, then remembered that Mexicans and their descendents have been involved in the agriculture of northern Colorado for about 150 years. The area is nearly treeless, with some cotton-woods marking the watercourses and only a few planted conifers or willows near ranch houses.

There were traces of snow alongside the road, lots of green fields and, at one point, a crop duster at work in the vicinity of the Homestead Bible Camp and Kiowa Church. I saw a few broken dreams out here, windowless houses surrounded by huge trees that had been skinny saplings when they were built, and I wondered about the people who'd built them and then moved on. It seemed to me that I had done a great deal of that myself.

At Wiggins, CO, near the junction of CO 52 and I-76, I saw a most welcome sign, "Rest Area" and stopped to deliver the morning's coffee. I followed I-76 for a short way and remembered that I hadn't liked it in the past because it was a concrete highway with asphalt seams. It had the kind of surface that causes tires to go "snick, snick" like the wheels of a railroad train, only it's much more annoying. It's still concrete and I still don't like it. Besides, there's a railroad embankment on one side that limits the view to the south.

After only a few miles, I got off I-76 for US 34 to enter Fort Morgan, the boyhood home of Glen Miller. Fort Morgan was established in 1864-1865, and built by "galvanized rebels", Confederate prisoners who were allowed to enlist to fight Indians in the West. It was named for Col. Christopher A. Morgan, U. S. Volunteers, about whom little else is known.

By now, I wondered why I had been in so many "Forts". Sure, from Michener's "Centennial" I knew about the Sand Creek Massacre and the Arapahoe and Cheyenne on the warpath. And, yes, I'd seen any number of movies that portrayed courageous Southerners fighting in Yankee uniform, (their poster boy was Ben Johnson as Sergeant Tyree), but was all that stuff really FACT? Yes. Also I know that in December 1866, up in Wyoming, Captain William J. Fetterman fell for the Indian ruse of a hasty retreat and led his men into an ambush that wiped them out. He has been immortalized in dozens of movies where brash young officers have done the same. Art imitates life.

In Brush, CO, or maybe it was Fort Morgan, (in all honesty I found little to distinguish prairie towns from one another) I stopped to replenish my water supply with a six-pack and then left behind all signs of agriculture as the prairie turned to sagebrush and yucca. I passed several large feedlots, seeing them before I smelled them thanks to a tailwind.

After passing through Akron, CO, a city that will not earn a prize for its main street, I found the USDA Agricultural Research Station in the middle of nowhere. Once upon a time, when selling laboratory equipment and supplies, I had traveled all the way out here, only to ring up a "No Sale". Seeing it again reminded me that I had consoled myself with the better part of a six-pack of beer on the drive home.

Otis, CO is typical of many of the towns I encountered. Once known as "one-horse towns" they are now "one-light towns"; they have a single traffic light at their major intersection, if they're lucky enough to have a major intersection. My town, Bandon, has one major intersection, but three traffic lights, the third having been installed since I moved there, a sure sign of progress. Anyway, Otis had homes with a neat and tidy appearance along the main street, as did Yuma, another decent town.

Outside Yuma, there's a turnout designated as the "Yuma Washout". "Now, what the hell is a washout?" I wondered. Well, that's where all the cattle trucks pull in to get washed out after discharging their loads. It's got to be done somewhere and, sure enough, across the road was a feedlot with, not just plain hamburger on the hoof, but in this case, prime sirloin on the hoof– sleek, fat cattle.

Eckley, CO looked as though it had been forgotten by the world, with rusting farm machinery, boarded up windows everywhere and un-harvested corn in the fields. Despite the 1st Pioneer National Bank's time-temperature clock, Wray, CO won't win any awards, either. Somewhere along the way, I noted that the towns seemed to be about 12 to 15 miles apart and wondered why there was such a consistent distance. More on that later.

I entered Nebraska after passing the town of Laird, CO. Nebraska, "The Good Life, Home of Arbor Day". The land became less arid, there were a lot more watercourses and cottonwood trees and the horizon suddenly came closer.

When I crossed the Arikaree River I saw cultivated farmland again to my right, and open prairie to my left, an interesting contrast. By now I was driving in shirtsleeves, my air conditioner working, with an outside temperature of 64 degrees, a marked contrast to November in Utah and Wyoming.

It was windy, though, and tumbleweeds as large as three feet in diameter were blowing across the highway; when necessary, I gave them the right of way. I tuned the radio to 93.9, Coyote Country, because a billboard had said they carried Rush and Dr. Laura, and I needed a laugh. Rush did not disappoint me.

As I crossed a county line, a sign said I was entering the Central Time Zone and shortly thereafter, another sign pointed the way to the Visitor Center at Massacre Canyon. There was a sculpture in the shape of an Indian with a lance and a buffalo, so I assumed that the canyon was a place where the buffalo were driven over a cliff and then harvested, hence "massacre". My research later showed Massacre Canyon was the location of a fight between the Sioux and Pawnee, where 156 Pawnee men, women and children were trapped and slaughtered by their fellow Native Americans. Ten more than at Wounded Knee, but nobody ever wrote "Bury My Heart at Massacre Canyon". I wonder why not?

Thinking about Rush, politics and Wounded Knee gave rise to some thoughts about Political Correctness. Personally, I regard PC as a form of insidious mind control. I believe there is a minority of Americans who wish to force the rest of us to conform in word, deed and perhaps even thought, to whatever agenda they have. They are, in their own way, no different from the Nazi and Communist parties that enforced conformist policies in their day. People have lost jobs, and perhaps more, merely for voicing their personal opinions of others. I'm afraid it will get worse, because seldom are the champions of such policies the actual "downtrodden masses" they are seeking to protect. They seem to have unlimited sources of money, too.

There used to be a time when Americans could laugh at themselves, and at each other. When I was growing up my city was composed of ethnic neighborhoods, carryovers from when immigrants clustered among their own people. Catholic churches were named after patron saints of European countries and sermons were delivered in native tongues. Despite these seemingly divisive factors, kids grew up as Americans, and were thrust into the melting pot in schools where they learned to defend their respective heritages with fists and humor. Instead of sensitivity training we learned to grow a thick skin.

I tend to trust only members of my own generation, you know. Don't lecture me about PC, or any other subject, unless you can name Vaughn Monroe's theme song. I really don't trust anyone who doesn't know who Vaughn Monroe was.

Were Susan here to comment, she would merely smile and nod and call me Brother Pontificus. Again.

I had a number of other random thoughts as I drove the roads towards Grand Island, NE and my room for the night:

- It was fun playing dodge ball with a big tumbleweed.

- I paid in advance for gas at Casey's General Store, but didn't have to; people are more trusting and honest once you leave the metropolitan areas.

- Cambridge, NE has a population of only 1,000, but they have a hospital, lots of big houses and tall trees.

- Atlanta, NE is home of a WWII German POW camp, pop 134, the town, not the camp. I don't know the camp's pop. Zero, I hope.

- There aren't very many Mexican restaurants in Nebraska, but there are plenty of John Deere dealerships.

- I passed Funk, NE and it wasn't blue.

- Minden, NE (I lived in Minden, NV for a while, stayed overnight for a week in Minden, LA and now found another Minden) is the home of Pioneer Village, which had been advertising lots of antiques, cars and now advertised the first plane to fly airmail.

And finally, after leaving US 34, I reached Grand Island, NE, where I found a Days Inn, a Red Lobster and a mall to crawl.

COLUMBIA

Vaughn Monroe's theme song, by the way, was "Racing With The Moon."

As I left Grand Island in near darkness, the low-hanging clouds were illuminated from beneath in a glorious pre-dawn show. US 34, signed in one direction as the Henry Fonda Memorial Highway is called in the other, the Husker Highway. It turns out that Henry Fonda was born in Grand Island; I don't know how long he stayed. I skirted the downtown area and got out of town very quickly, dodging the rush hour of the 42,000 souls who call Grand Island home.

A grand island, indeed, if it can even be called that. As nearly as I can tell, the Platte River, a relatively small stream to begin with, divides into a number of what I'd call rivulets and comes together again at some point downstream of Grand Island. Perhaps in the olden days there was more water, a more pronounced island, but today the Platte was only a trickle. (News reports six months after my visit said a tremendous rainstorm dropped over seven inches of rain in a 24-hour period, and caused some serious flooding. I was guilty of contempt prior to investigation.)

I saw Angus cattle feeding in the stubble of a corn-field and wondered if that's what they mean by corn-fed beef. Then I recalled that the expressions are "corn-fed hogs" and "grain-fed beef". And then I recalled that hogs are mostly up in Iowa, where I wasn't going this trip, so I forgot the whole thing.

Towns in Colorado and Nebraska seemed to be situated about 12 miles apart. Just as one grain elevator, or silo, or whatever they call the grain storage structures out here (being a man, I refused to stop and ask) fades in the rear view mirror, another pops up in the windshield. When I mentioned it, Mary Ellen emailed me to tell me that 12 miles was just about the distance a wagon train could travel in a day and that people would just say, "This is it," and stop to settle. It's as good a theory as any. I thought the distance might have had something to do with the railroads.

Anyway, I had been to a local shopping mall in Grand Island the evening before and half the people I saw…well, OK, maybe quite a few…well, lots anyway, were wearing Nebraska Cornhusker gear. The waitress in the Red Lobster had said that she expected a quiet night because there was a local high school playoff. On a Monday night. Opposite the Vikings and Colts on TV. Sure do love their football in Nebraska. And, judging by the signs I saw for NASCAR collectibles, so do they love their racing as well. Outdoor sports fare well there.

There were some well-kept properties in Aurora, NE and the ubiquitous trailer park at the edge of town. At York, I took US 81 south to Kansas with the intention of then heading east to Missouri.

While driving east just after sunrise, the sun had been just behind my rear view mirror; if it had been a little to one side, I could not have blocked it with a visor and would have been blinded. This was like the one smear that the windshield wiper makes that is dead level with your line of vision, a law of nature, but this time, working FOR me for a change. I was grateful.

As I left Nebraska I noted that cornfields had been in abundance. Right to Life signs had been, too.

US 81 was much like a freeway, four lanes with a median strip, and boring. The land began to flatten as I approached Kansas and I was much tempted to head towards Independence, MO and pay my respects to Mr. Truman. I decided not to, though, crossed the Little Blue River, which was much bigger than the Big Blue River and reached Belleville, where I turned east on US 36.

Mr. Truman, I think, is much to be admired as the President who made two of the most difficult decisions of the Twentieth Century. He gave the order to drop the atomic bomb on Japan, and he fired General Douglas MacArthur. Regardless of one's position on either question, you have to give the guy credit for making a decision, doing the job he was getting paid for, and not relying on pollsters to tell him which way the political winds were blowing. If that's all there were to it, I could be President.

In the years since 1945, there have been many apologists for the actions we took at Hiroshima and Nagasaki. There is not a single shred of belief in me that, had the situation been reversed, the Japanese would have hesitated to use the bomb on us. I doubt they would be apologizing to us today if they had. And had they won the war, we would be their economic slaves, in a different sense from the way we are today. Trade with Japan continues to be a one-way street and their samurais now prowl the boardrooms of their corporations instead of the decks of their aircraft carriers. I chuckle when I hear Americans called "racists". The Japanese could teach the Ku Klux Klan a thing or two about racism.

I was now traveling through rolling terrain, heavily wooded in the many river bottoms and not as flat as the Kansas I'd expected. The fields were green; there were cows in the corn, but no sheep in the meadow. I passed through Munden, KS, not Minden, and still enjoyed rolling country, prairie without sagebrush and wooded areas in the bottoms and hilltops. There was a lot of uncultivated land out here, and I thought it strange in view of the apparent abundance of water.

As I approached Marysville, KS, US 36 became the Pony Express Highway, and in Marysville itself, where I had to wait for two trains going in opposite directions to cross the main street, there was a sign advertising Historic Pony Express Station #1. Well, that sign led me to believe that the Pony express started here, but some research showed that it started in St. Joseph, MO, just like all the wagon trains did. Marysville was probably a relay station.

Outside Seneca, KS, I saw a series of signs in the old Burma Shave fashion that read:

> Nothing was
> As cold and shivery
> As a moonlight run
> To an outdoor privy
> Reminisce

I wonder who put that up?

Fairview, KS bills itself as the home of General Bernard W. Rogers, whoever he was. Well, he was a fellow West Pointer, that's who he was, rising to the position of Supreme Commander of NATO in 1979. I guess we missed each other in the service.

As I reached St. Joseph the woods got thicker and the leaves took on more color, a sure indication of hardwoods. I crossed the wide Missouri thinking, "Ain't so wide…" In St. Joe US 36 became a freeway and, outside of town, more like an Interstate, so I left it, turning south on US 65 at Chillicothe, and headed towards Carrollton to pick up I-70 to Columbia. US 36 had been the VFW Highway, now US 65 was the American Legion Highway, and here I passed an Amish horse and buggy, a pacifist on a military memorial road.

I crossed the Missouri again on this southbound leg and also crossed US 24, which, I believe, goes through

Colorado Springs and up around Pike's Peak. Along the route I saw an old fashioned street light with no lamp and a sign saying "Back Yonder". I took that to be directions to, or the name of, someone's residence, and I recalled that Susan used to call Bandon the "back o' beyond".

Upon entering Marshall, MO, I saw the ubiquitous John Deere dealership on the edge of town and realized that every town worth its salt has one. The countryside looked so much like rural New York or New Jersey to me that I thought to myself, "Toto, we're definitely not in Kansas anymore."

When I crossed the Missouri for the third time, I noted steep cliffs on the east side and a substantial flood-plain, and spotted a sign for historic downtown Rocheport. The spot is identified in William Clark's journal, notable for Indian paintings and carvings in the limestone rock that also contained flints. The Corps of Discovery discovered rattlesnakes there as well and killed three of them. I didn't stop to check for more.

There are a few place names in Missouri that in-trigued me. I saw a sign for Sedalia and, besides Sedalia, CO, I think I've seen a few other Sedalias in the country. Someday, I'll look up the origin of that name. The origin of Lake Lottawanna is no mystery, though, probably named by a guy with a grasping wife and a passel of kids.

I finally found Columbia, which I had been mentally referring to as Columbia, South Carolina, because that's the only Columbia I've ever been in, and a Fairfield Inn for the night. On the morrow I would pick up my daughter Claire at the airport and cross, for the first time ever in a car, the Mississippi River.

QUINCY

        Storms that had delivered snow to the Western states, were catching up with me as I drove east. That meant that, sooner or later, I'd encounter rain. In the meantime, though, it was 58 degrees under a high and thin overcast, and a really pleasant day as I drove southward to Jefferson City on US 63. Along the way, I began to notice brick or brick-faced houses for the first time.

        Although the ground was green with grass and other growth, the trees had lost their leaves in Missouri. I thought that I'd like to see this country in springtime, when the trees are fleshed out with leaves and flowers are blooming, and then I remembered that Susan and I had flown into St. Louis and driven down to Alabama in May a few years back, and the country had been lushly green.

        Anyone who has traveled as far as I had by this point is sure to have noticed a rich variety of road kills. Back in Oregon I had seen a substantial number of dead deer, and noted dead coyotes in the desert, but out in Nebraska, Kansas and now, Missouri, there were an abundance of raccoons, groundhogs, squirrels and, of course, skunks. The recipes for Road Kill Stew are endless in America.

        Someone had asked me via email if I were homesick yet, and I had replied, "No." I was weeping for Susan daily in the car, but I probably would have cried even more if I had been at home. Being with people was stemming the flow of tears. I suppose that those who had known her chose to mourn her in silence. Those who had not, merely expressed their condolences and moved the conversations along. It seems that, beyond wakes and memorials, there is little to say about the dead until time has passed, or else, like me, people don't know what to say.

As for home, there were, at this point, a lot of people I had yet to see and was looking forward to seeing, and the desire to meet with them was overshadowing any thoughts of home. I was going to meet with some people I hadn't seen in 46 years. Imagine that! "Once I get to California, and turn north," I thought, "Then I'll think about home."

I saw a domed building on the skyline at about the same time I passed a sign for "Capitol View" and figured out that Jefferson City must be the capitol of Missouri. I have long ago forgotten the litany of our states' capitols, but in a moment of mischievousness I couldn't help but wonder if Jefferson City had been named for Thomas or for some popular basketball player.

Shortly before entering Jefferson City I turned off on MO 94, to get back on a blue highway. I was following the Missouri River valley on that road, with cliffs to my left and a large floodplain and the river to my right. As I tried to coin a word to describe the cliffs, like Stratificationalism or Sedimentationalism, neither of which can get past the spell checker of my word processing software, I spotted another road kill and thought, "My God, how could I have forgotten to mention possum?"

There were cultivated fields to my right, now, the river was a long way off and out of view. At Tebbets, MO there was a grain elevator and a post office and little else. No doubt the farmers visit 'town' for their mail. On my left, between the road and the cliffs there was a graded embankment and signs pointing to the Katy Trail. I had to look that one up and found that the Missouri-Kansas-Texas Railroad, Katy for short, stopped running in 1986 and its roadbed was converted into a hiking/biking trail. Here, in the river bottoms, it wound through Missouri's wine-producing area, called Rhineland or Weinstrasse. I didn't see a soul on the trail.

MO 94 follows the Lewis and Clark trail, and there was a lot of evidence that I was in Middle America. FFA signs were everywhere, for you city folk that is Future Farmers of America, usually a high school club/organization for the kids who want to take farming seriously. I take farming seriously; I regard it as one of America's noblest professions.

Out in the middle of nowhere, I saw a red barn with a little sign saying, "Support our Troops". And later, in an exercise of double doming, I wondered, after seeing the sign for Little Tavern Creek Road, if there really is a little tavern, if there's a Big Tavern Creek, if there's a Middle Tavern Creek Road, and so on. The scenery wasn't really that boring, but I think I was getting a little saddle sore and needed some kind of mental exercise.

The road left the floodplain several times to climb forested hills and it crossed a few one-lane bridges (Yield to Oncoming Traffic. Well, how the hell do you do that if the other guy is reading the same sign on his side? Prime opportunity to play Chicken?) It diverged at one point to go to Starkenburg or Rhineland, leading me to wonder about the ancestry of the original settlers. Not for long, because a harvest machine was raising dust that the wind carried across the road und der hausfraus vill have to sveep der doorsteps in Rhineland.

People out here have their sense of humor, though. I saw a variation of the dummy witch slammed into a tele-phone pole. This one had a sign that said, "Don't drink and fly." Further down the road a pair of camouflage-clad legs with boots protruded from the center of a hay roll. Amusing stuff.

Later, I found Lost Creek.

The road became hilly with a lot of twists and turns and I couldn't look around a lot. That was fortunate, because a kamikaze ground squirrel made a bid to become road kill and I toed the brake and missed him. I came down to river level again and pulled over at a picnic table turnoff to stretch, look at the river and check the map. This was the first time I had ever been afoot on the banks of the Missouri and at this point it was quite wide and flowing strongly. "I wouldn't want to paddle across that," I thought, and got back into the car and drove on. There's something to say about the perspective of seeing a river from its banks versus crossing over it on a highway bridge.

Even out in this ultra-rural area I saw a Waste Management truck. They're everywhere, people, and they're reading our garbage. Beware.

There had been many signs referring to the Lewis & Clark expedition. Merry and Bill had been very busy in this area, but now there was also a sign for the Daniel Boone Monument. I knew that Boone had spent his final years in Missouri, somewhere on the river, but I had to look up some facts. I still don't know what the Daniel Boone Monument is, but the Daniel Boone Home (where he really didn't live) is in Defiance, not far off MO 94. Daniel died 14 miles away, in Marthasville, was buried, then supposedly dug up by people from Frankfort, KY and transported there. "Supposedly" is because the remains later dug up in Kentucky proved to be those of a large black man, not Boone. Where he is today, is anyone's guess.

I passed now through vineyards, the village of Dutzow, whose houses came right up to the street, and lots of Halloween decorations still out on November 10th. I saw a sign on a church, "Sign Broken, Message Inside," and blessed the pastor for his sense of humor.

There was a vine growing in some places that I thought to be kudzu, but wondered if I were too far north for it. Sure enough, a little research on the Internet told me that kudzu is used in Missouri as a roadside ground cover, although in this case, I think it was growing wild.

I reached civilization, crossed the Missouri one more time, made my way to the St. Louis airport and picked up my daughter, Claire for the trip to her home in Quincy, IL.

Claire had been visiting her sister in Denver. She is my oldest child, excuse me, my oldest daughter, a woman of forty-one. Although she and Stephanie had spent a good number of their early years at odds, and can still snarl at each other from time to time, the crisis of cancer had awakened the right responses and she had rushed to be at her sister's side during chemo and hospitalization.

We succeeded in finding one another in the St. Louis airport. It was a real mess, under construction and with detours everywhere. Without cell phones we might have missed one another forever. We got out of St. Louis, and went north on US 61 through few farms and mostly wooded terrain to Hannibal, MO. There, we crossed the Mississippi (ain't so wide) and went on up to Quincy. I had dinner downtown with Claire and her husband, Jack, and strolled to Washington Park, the site of several debates between Lincoln and Douglas. I had always KNOWN that someday I would walk in Lincoln's footsteps.

ILLIANA

Claire and I enjoyed breakfast at a down-home Quincy restaurant, with blue and white-checked tablecloths and good coffee. After breakfast we toured the downtown and the Mississippi River waterfront areas. Quincy is full of grand old brick houses, mostly converted to apartments these days, and the river area is composed of older buildings, not being restored, but grand in their air of permanence and venerability. It's a really picturesque place.

When I left Quincy my destination was someplace; anyplace I could spend the night before continuing on to Grandville, MI and a visit with my oldest stepson, Adam, and his family. I decided to use the blue highways of Illinois and Indiana to get there. I thought about going to the campuses (campi?) of Purdue in Lafayette and Notre Dame in South Bend to troll for coeds, but P.D. discouraged me from doing this. P.D. is my little inner friend, Prudence Dictates, who tries to keep me out of trouble. Susan was fond of talking about Sally Forth and Gay Abandon, but I always regarded them as rather militant. P.D. is gentle and wise and, though I might not always listen to her, she catches more flies with honey than the others do with vinegar.

The area north of St. Louis had been heavily wooded, so too was Illinois for a while. The homes and the woods made me feel that I was officially back East, not just because I'd crossed the Mississippi, but also because the architecture and flora were very much like the area where I grew up. I was amazed, though, at how many homes in the country, either manufactured or stick-built, had a front door that wasn't used, often without a path to it, sometimes even without steps. If people are going to always use the garage or back door, why bother to put a front door on the place?

(Yes, I know, Building Codes, but if George Carlin asked the question, you'd laugh.)

I drove along state highways from Quincy to Lafayette. Along the route, I had cloudy skies with no rain, but saw the Wrath of God off to the south, my right as I was driving. The feared storms had caught up with me, but were now passing to the south and I was glad. For a change, I drove through gently rolling terrain with towns 12 miles apart, ubiquitous grain elevators and cornfields. By the way, I love that word, ubiquitous. After learning what it means I wrote about a trip to Arizona and described its "ubiquitous escarpments". I was teased about that phrase ever after.

I reached the town of Camp Point and the Bastert Farm Equipment Co. formed my first impression. It had every conceivable piece of farm equipment on display, some used, some new, right next to a bunch of wrecked racing cars. The town of 1,300 souls had neat white homes with well-manicured lawns; it was a very nice looking town but for the junk out at the edge. So much for first impressions.

By now I realized that many of the farmers working the fields on this cold November morning were in cammies and I had to wonder what they were hiding from. Perhaps cammies are the "in" fashion in rural Middle America. Perhaps they are the warmest clothes the farmers own. Perhaps they get only limited use during the hunting season and the guys want to get their money's worth. Perhaps I should get some cammies and shut up.

At about that point I realized that I was seeing shutters on the windows of homes, albeit decorative ones, and wondered when they had begun to appear. I know shutters are not a big thing out West, although I've seen some in Oregon, and I know they are a "must" in the Northeast. Anyway, I was in Shutterland.

Occasionally I encountered some monstrous farm vehicles on the road. They usually pulled over to allow traffic to pass, but I had no idea whatsoever what they were used for. My ignorance of farming methods is exceeded only by my misunderstanding of women.

After crossing the Illinois River, filled with some pretty big barges, I reached Havana, IL, which was completely lined with large American flags. Well, of course, it was Veterans' Day. They did it proud.

Outside of town: more corn.

Heyworth, IL, looked as though it might be an interesting place for a future visit. Its sign said it is the home of the Simpkins War Museum. Since I had never heard of the Simpkins War, I thought I had better check it out on the Internet. Seems the Simpkins War Museum is the private collection of war memorabilia from the Civil, Spanish-American, WWI, WWII, Korean, Vietnam and Gulf Wars and belongs to the mayor of Heyworth, Gary Simpkins. It's closed from October to April and then only open from 1-4 on Saturdays and Sundays. On second thought, I'll pass.

Fisher, IL has Fisher High School, "Home of the Bunnies and the Scotties". Boy, I don't want to touch that one. Outside of Fisher, a home had a hideous mail box modeled after a bass whose mouth opened to accept mail; it's shape and iridescent colors were reminiscent of the "Billy Bass" singing wall trophy. I had never seen anything that stupid, and I desperately want one just like it.

At the state line, I crossed the Wabash River and entered Indiana, where the first sign I saw was "Get America Out of the UN". Hmmm. My kind of people. The roads were wet and as I turned onto IN 28, the George Rogers Clark Memorial Highway, the car started to spin out, but I remembered how to turn the wheels to control a spin and I executed a nice piece of driving.

The remainder of the drive to Lafayette was unremarkable.

I left Lafayette the next morning after not having looked for Purdue, and leisurely drove eastward in sunshine. The houses I passed were all set well back from the road and all had neat emerald lawns. The contrast with the previous day's driving was marked.

As I drove through Indiana, I recalled that I had given the state some pretty bad press after passing through it a few years before with Susan. On that trip we had gone through some rather poor looking farmland; even the Amish farms, normally remarkable for their excellent husbandry, appeared to be run-down. When I drove through the state this time, I was impressed by the pride of ownership exemplified by the people whose farms and towns I saw. Either there is a significant difference between the regions of Indiana I traveled through on the two occasions, or else word of my comments had gotten back to the state and they cleaned up their act.

The other fact that impressed me while driving in Indiana was that, since leaving Weld County, CO I had driven over 1,000 miles and seen nothing but productive farmland. It was staggering, and still is, to think about how much food this country produces, and how it could produce even more.

This was the first time I had driven across America. To realize that I had only seen a narrow corridor and that the productivity extended for 500 miles to either side was truly unbelievable. I may have moaned about unchanging scenery, about watching cornfield after cornfield go by, but I have to put the breadbasket of America on a par with the Grand Canyon as one of America's wonders. In a word, I was impressed.

The day saw me go through a number of towns, neat for the most part, but unimpressive nevertheless; I was beginning to get a little tired of the blue highways. Perhaps I felt the pressures of a schedule and believed I didn't have the time to really poke my nose into those places that deserved a good nose poking. It was frustrating.

In Logansport, a larger town than most, I saw the Federal Mogul Company plant and wondered who the hell they were. After researching, I found that Federal Mogul is a large OEM and aftermarket manufacturer of parts for automobiles, mainly power train and sealing systems parts. It is in bankruptcy, due largely to asbestos litigation, another victim of lawsuits.

I will not claim that asbestos lawsuits are frivolous. However it seems to me that the government, in an effort to achieve a balance of trade, could consider exporting some of our lawyers to a country where the per capita count of attorneys is lower than in the United States, like, for instance, EVERYWHERE ELSE in the world.

Logansport reminded me very much of Providence, RI where I grew up. The architecture was the same, old factories were closed down, and the Eel River, a shallow stream, reminded me of the Woonasquatucket River. I extricated myself from the town and went north on IN 25 where I saw a sign for "Inniquity, A Country Inn." That begged the question, so I looked up "iniquity" in my Webster's and found it meant, "want of moral principle". I wanna go to Inniquity. Preferably with a female friend.

Shortly after that a church sign read, "Read the Bible, Free Gift Inside". I liked that phrase, but I like "Inniquity" better.

In the town of Rochester, I had my oil changed at a family run business and marveled at how much nicer everyone was than at the places in Los Angeles. There, the kids who service you today will not still be there in three months when you come back, so why should they care? While waiting, I noticed that Indiana license plates carry www.in.gov in case you want to know more about the state.

Then, at some point northbound I realized that a guy had been tailgating me for about two miles. I varied my speed, but he remained the same distance behind me, and I concluded that he had his mind on something else, and was on autopilot. In this, the Information Age, we are bombarded with so much information through so many kinds of media that many of us just don't pay attention to driving. Pay attention. Spencer Tracy said that many times in "Northwest Passage" and it still rings true.

Random thoughts as I continued north:

- Farmland began to give way to more and more forest.

- Honkers Family Restaurant had geese on their sign. Of course.

- I had dinner at a Chinese restaurant in Lafayette and the fortune cookie, to which I usually add the words "in bed" at the end, said, "You will have wonderful surprises over the next few months (in bed)" and as I write, the few months are up and I'm still waiting.

- I saw the Golden Dome of Notre Dame and wondered if they had any Irish students.

- Some flags were at half-staff and I hoped they weren't for Yassar Arafat, who had just died.

- Paw Paw, MI is the home of the Julian Winery.

- Down the road from Paw Paw I saw the first hog farms I'd encountered on the trip.

And with that, I reached Grandville and the home of Adam and Cyndi.

ROCHESTER

I left Grandville on a frosty Monday morning after a pleasant weekend with Adam, Cyndi, Camron and Meghan. Adam was the oldest of Susan's children, and since he had been 15 when he came to America he still has a pronounced British accent. He enlisted in the Air Force from high school and is the only one of the four boys to take on American citizenship. He continues to serve his new country with a hospital unit in the Air Force Reserve, and was called up for the Iraq war, and again for Hurricane Katrina. Adam's Reserve duty on the previous weekend had provided another constraint in planning my trip.

After meeting and marrying in the snow swept plains of Minot, North Dakota, Adam and Cyndi left the Air Force and moved to Grandville, near the town where Cyndi grew up. During my stay, Camron, age 8, had clung to me frequently, probably because I was the link to his departed and beloved Grandmum.

I was particularly grateful to Adam for having taken over some of the duties attending to Susan during the last few weeks of her life. Susan had determined to fight her disease to the end, and I had committed to supporting her belief that she could win, even when her wasting body and mind signaled otherwise. Just when I was about to throw in the towel and suggest that she might want to see her sons, Susan told me to call Adam.

When he arrived, Adam pitched in and took care of his mother, slept in shifts with me and freed me to obtain the necessary medical supplies for her care. His devotion to his mum will endear him to me forever.

Now, driving south on a road very much like a free-way, I decided to "make time" that day. Being a guest again had been fine, and would be again. And again. But I felt that I needed a little time to myself, that going from one person's house to the next could become a bit hectic. I was determined to stay overnight in a hotel in the Buffalo area, if possible, and just do as I damn well pleased. In the mean-time the eastern sky turned from a brilliant crimson to sky blue pink, my favorite color.

Passing through Battle Creek, MI I remembered that it was the place to which I mailed my cereal box tops to get a Lone Ranger Atom Bomb Ring or a deed to one square inch of the Yukon, patrolled by Sgt Preston and his wonder dog, King. If I had had the foresight to save either of those items, I think I could make a lot of money today. "Hi, Ho Silver," and "On, King, On You Huskies," indeed.

Somewhere on the road I saw a tractor-trailer with the trailer collapsed in the center so that it made a big V. I'd seen jack-knifed trailers and overturned ones before, but never one like that. Fortunately, it was on the shoulder of the road. Items like that kept me awake, because driving this road was rather dull. Let me refer you to my three-page book, "America From the Freeways". Snore.

I swung south on US 23 towards Ohio and Toledo, a road I probably had traveled once when on a training trip for Kodak in 1971. As cars passed me I noticed that Michigan plates had a lot of different kinds of decorative emblems on the left side, something I found distracting in case I wanted to remember a plate number from an accident or something. Was this another sign of advancing senility? Or more anal behavior?

After crossing the Maumee River, I saw a sign for Bowling Green University, one of those college names I remembered from the Prudential Football Scoreboard. Years ago the PFS used to report all the scores of college games, even Slippery Rock's; nowadays TV seems obsessed with the

Top Ten or Top Twenty. That leaves alumni of the rest to watch for scores on the Internet or in the newspaper. And that, of course, is the result of what some TV executives think that young, upwardly mobile men with spendable income will want to see and so they gear their advertising appropriately.

In high school I tried out for baseball (and failed) and tried out for track (and failed) and didn't worry too much about the stigma of failure, because other guys were trying out and failing, too. We just weren't good enough to make the team and that's all there was to it.

There didn't seem to be much emphasis on being Number 1 then; I didn't think I needed a guarantee of success before trying something. Not that I didn't worry about not succeeding, everyone did, there just wasn't the pressure that there seems to be today. It seems to me that I was in college, studying psychology before I ever heard the phrase "self-esteem", and it never bothered me that I hadn't been handed any in school.

I cannot for the life of me tell you which college football team was number one last year and with this year's bowl games over, I'm not sure who made it this year, either. That sort of thing is just not important to me, never was.

Speaking of advertising, I think we all know that the industry pays a great deal of attention to ratings, polls, surveys, and such to find out who is watching what. Companies that want to get their messages to the right people will buy time on the programs that those people watch. But I have to wonder if TV executives might not be willing to alter program content in order to appeal to Big Money, and whether or not TV News, for example, is slanted to attract watchers who are prime prospects for Big Advertisers. Is the tail wagging the dog? Some people feel that network news programs have a liberal bent, and I wonder if this is the reason.

All that because of Bowling Green. Hmmpff.

The Ohio Turnpike surprised me. Other toll roads I've been on, and were yet to get on during this trip, print the toll fees for each exit on the ticket. This can help the driver and/or passenger get the proper fee ready before exiting. Not so the Ohio Turnpike. No fees printed. Make a guess. Fumble for your wallet. This stinks, and I resolved that, in the future, I shall be taking my turnpike business elsewhere.

I exited the Turnpike as soon as practicable and used I-90 to head towards Cleveland. I passed through Elyria, where I had once stayed with Susan on a trip in the other direction, and then through Cleveland, about which the less said the better. I will say that the Cuyahoga River looked as though it could catch fire again, but also that Lake Erie was beautifully blue as I passed the site of the old Municipal Stadium. The lake looked quite large and I wondered if it was as big as the Pacific. Why not? You can't see the other side of either of them.

Pennsylvania welcomed me with a never-ending procession of trees on either side of the Interstate and with an occasional glimpse of the very blue Lake Erie. The forty-five minutes or so that I spent in Pennsylvania was the least amount of time I spent in any state on the entire trip. I think I was in Maryland on the Delmarva Peninsula for a longer time.

New York welcomed me with vineyards, green grass on the freeway verge, some trees and long, low hills to the south. I saw a sign for "Niagara Falls – 34 Miles", and wondered how long people had been calling it Viagra Falls. Probably since the day after Viagra was introduced, maybe even before.

I reached Amherst, NY, on the eastern side of Buffalo and hunkered down for the night in a Choice hotel, in this case, a Sleep Inn. I had discovered in Lafayette that the Choice hotel chain was offering a free night for every two nights spent during the period November 1 to December 31. Why not take advantage?

As I left Amherst the next morning, headed north towards NY 31, I crossed over what I thought to be the Erie Canal. Not so! It seems the 363-mile Erie Canal, completed in 1825, had gotten a "makeover" in 1917 to become the New York State Barge Canal. It follows the same route as the Erie Canal, roughly, but when I lived in upstate New York, I don't recall anyone ever calling it the Barge Canal. Naturally, signs abound along the way referring to it as the Erie, so as to garner historical credits, I suppose. Anyway, at this point, people had houses and docks right on the canal's edge. All the way to Fairport, NY, my next destination, I was to cross and re-cross the Erie Canal.

In the midst of all the billboards for attractions at Viagra Falls, I noticed a sign designating North Tonawanda, NY as the home of the carousel. I also noticed a lot of people doing "California stops" at stop signs and red lights. I began to think that a lot of the things I blame on Californians as far as driving habits are concerned are really national in scope, but mainly in the major metro areas. I guess it's the metro traffic that breeds the bad habits. You're welcome, California.

At first attracted to a huge country barn, brightly painted with "Antiques" posted over the door, I decided that it looked too touristy for my taste. Then I saw an old faded red barn with a barely readable sign saying "Chew Mail Pouch Tobacco", and it seemed more authentic than the "Dr. Kilmer's Swamp Root" barn down in Langlois, OR. So I checked it out on the Internet.

It seems the Mail Pouch Tobacco Company, formed in 1879, began painting barns in the 1920s and stopped in 1992 when it changed ownership. Supposedly, over 20,000 barns had been painted and many of them re-painted. There are folks with Internet sites who make a hobby of seeking out, and photographing, Mail Pouch barns throughout Appalachia and the Midwest. As far as I'm concerned, if you've seen one…

When I reached NY 31, I discovered that it was named Saunders Settlement Road. I got about 150 hits on the Internet, and learned that many of them were just addresses of businesses or schools. The rest of them, though, were about lawsuits involving someone named Saunders, so maybe the name came from a big trial. Only in America.

I reached Lockport, a pleasant enough town with a dead factory, in this case General Motors, and noticed that people had swept their downed leaves out into the street. I'd forgotten that in the East, leaf collection is a municipal chore. It occurred to me that there was no such thing in Bandon and that, come spring, I'd have to rake my leaves to rehabilitate my lawn, but since there was nothing I could do at the moment, I refused to worry about it.

My next two towns would be Gasport and Middleport, and I remembered that my hero, William Least Heat-Moon, had traveled down the Erie Canal as one leg of his cross-country journey by water. If memory serves, he called it the Erie, not the Barge, Canal in his book, "River Horse". He was going in the other direction.

In between towns Route 31 was just a row of neat, tidy homes alongside the road, and it was a long time before I noticed the first "For Sale" sign. When I saw it, I realized how accustomed I am to seeing "For Sale" signs in the West. Southern California is a volatile real estate market, for sure, Dude; but even in my little resort town of Bandon, signs are popping up constantly.

Driving up to a construction site in Medina, NY, I gave a little finger wave to the pretty gal conducting traffic and she sort of waved back. Then she stared after the car, as if to say, "Who was that Masked Man? Where was that car from? Do I know him?" She had a lot of blue eye shadow on, so she may have been both on the job and On The Hunt.

Medina, with angle-in parking on the main street, looked to have lots of potential as a shopping Mecca, but, although neat, most of the stores were conventional, rather than arts, crafts and gifts. They just aren't going to get any trendy kids from Buffalo to come out just for Florsheim shoes.

East of Medina, there was lots of un-harvested corn, and I was again staggered by the thought of the grain this country produces. I just couldn't get a grip on it. Still can't.

I bypassed downtown Albion and saw some lovely old two story homes on the outskirts of town. I thought that this was probably one of those places I drove through long ago when I lived in Rochester and intended to come back to and explore. I never did and probably never will. How many of those lost treasures are there in anyone's life?

Somewhere along the road a harvester was pouring grain into a dump truck, and here I had thought mid-November was too late for doing such things. I crossed over into Monroe County and noted that the Canal was full. I believe they drain it for the winter, but I could be mistaken. Again.

I decided to look up the old neighborhood and found The Bandit's, a country store we had used back in the 60s to avoid longer trips to the supermarket. We called it that because of the high prices the owner charged, although we got some beer there pretty cheap, Wiedemann's by name. The can looked so much like a Budweiser can, that we often fooled one another by holding one up at distance and inviting one over for "a Bud". The store was still in operation and hadn't yet been taken over by a 7-11.

The trees on Evergreen Drive had grown quite a bit and when I stopped to take some pictures of Ye Olde Homestead, the thought occurred to me that someone was going to accost me and ask what I was doing. Sure enough, the guy who bought the house from me drove up and asked.

I had never met the guy, but thought he was a jerk for having cut down the only tree in the back yard because of a tent moth infestation. I had saved the tree every spring by standing out in the cold and snow and slush and hosing it off to break up the nests before the caterpillars emerged. That saved the tree, only to have him cut it down. After meeting him, I became convinced he's a jerk.

I got away from that guy as soon as I could, knowing that he thinks I'm a jerk for having been so reserved and cool towards him, and started for downtown to meet Bob for lunch. Very little about North Chili (pronounced Chi-lie) had changed, very little about Rochester had changed. Lunch, however, was different and great.

POULTNEY

After a pleasant visit with Bob and Diane, lunch with a number of fellows Bob had mentioned in his emails and some I had met before, and introductions to some really splendid waitresses, I left Fairport for Vermont. There had been a very significant aspect to the stay in the Rochester area – no snow. The sky had been typically overcast, we'd had light drizzle, but the temperatures had been mild and that helped to dispel some of the gloom that I had always associated with the area since moving there in 1968.

On the way out of Fairport, I passed a farm on Turk Hill Road (where did they get that name?) and recalled that Bob had mentioned some kind of public outcry at the farmer who overpopulated his land. Seems he bred his sheep, but didn't sell or butcher any, and they were exceeding the land's capacity to support them. Well, that's his business, as far as I'm concerned, but ever since Walt Disney gave Bambi and his cohorts voices and emotions, there will be people who are bound to make his business, their business. There were also some critters that looked like llamas, but Bob had said they were alpacas and only he among all my friends is able to tell the difference.

Bob and I go back to the days when we were neighbors in 1969. Only his youngest child, Marci, was of an age to play with my children; his sons were a few years older. Bob had been in advertising and had moved from city to city as opportunities arose, and when his company in Rochester decided that his assistant could do his job for half the salary, he found himself unemployed.

I admired Bob greatly as he made the decision to go into business for himself, rather than to subject his family to another uprooting and move. He struggled during the early years, his wife went to work for the first time since college and discovered that she had a knack for banking, and they prospered, but paid a price. Like many married couples of our generation, their interests diverged, and they divorced. It was to happen to me a few years after.

Once Bob and I became single, we managed to visit one another. He came to Denver and Los Angeles when I lived there, but I always went to Rochester where he remained. We found one another dates and then re-married within a year of one another, but stayed in touch despite the distance. Bob had come to Bandon to spend some time with me in the early weeks after Susan's death, and I appreciated that beyond words.

Now, though, I was "Eastbound and down" on the New York State Thruway and stopped at the Clifton Springs rest area, where I paid $5.77 for a Cinnabon and orange juice. Welcome to New York. I really didn't want to drive on the Thruway, but, as I've mentioned, the time constraints of the trip forced me to take more than one high-speed, limited-access road.

So, too, did my complete and utter misjudgment of distances in the East. After thirty years in the West I had gotten used to looking at a map and estimating driving time according to the scale of Western states. I forgot that Rand McNally uses different scales for different states and that threw me off. I ended up using Interstates when I didn't need to, because I forgot Rule 1: Everything is closer in the East.

The Thruway was every bit as uninteresting as it had been nearly forty years before, when I first drove on it. A few sights served to provide amusement, though; for instance, I saw a guy reading a paper while driving, glancing up every few seconds to check the road. Read a sentence, check the road. Hit the ball, drag Harry. Real life can be funnier, or more tragic, than jokes.

There were a lot of waterfowl in the air; most were flying to the northwest. I surmised that they were headed for Lake Ontario, then onward to the Mississippi Flyway. Or something like that, I'm not an expert on waterfowl migratory patterns. Perhaps they, like me, were a little disoriented because they couldn't see the sun. I never did figure out which way was north while at Bob's house, later was told that it faces north.

Bob had mentioned a bit of a controversy regarding cultural diversity in his local school district and showed me an op-ed piece in the paper written by one of the teachers. It encouraged "diversity" without ever really defining it. I asked Bob if one of the cultures studied under this program was Multi-Generational Welfare, and he had no answer. Out West, it seemed, people were bending over backwards to flatter Asians and Hispanics who had absolutely no interest in a two-way street. So, are we encouraging "diversity" for the sake of the diverse, or just to make ourselves feel better? I don't particularly need more guilt; I was raised Catholic and deal with guilt almost as a way of life.

Eventually, I was driving down the Mohawk River Valley, with mountains to either side of me. It occurred to me that, as a kid, I had called them mountains, and so they are, in Vermont, New Hampshire and New York. But I have lived in the West for half my life, twelve of those years were spent in Colorado, and my viewpoint has changed considerably. I can only imagine how our pioneers, with the same perspective I had as a child, viewed the Rockies when they got there. The comparison is on a mind-boggling scale. It's said that Zebulon Pike, the intrepid explorer, told his men he was going to walk over to that "hill" on the horizon and staggered back into camp three days later, having not come a bit closer to the mountain that bears his name. So while I say "mountains", I was thinking "hills".

Anyway, the Mohawk Valley, named for the river, not the tribe, conjured up images of Henry Fonda and

Claudette Colbert braving the rigors of frontier life and fighting off Indians. Maybe I could have been a better long-distance runner in high school and college if I could have imagined some redskins chasing me as they chased Henry in that movie, but the thought never occurred to me back then.

In Yet Another Rest Stop (perhaps I should call the story of this journey YARS) I found a NY State Historical Sign referring to the Battle of Oriskany, at which General Herkimer had stopped a British invasion from the west. In fact what happened was that Herkimer was leading a group of Mohawk Valley militia to relieve the besieged Americans at Fort Stanwix when, surprise! He was ambushed by Indians. His force was decimated; Herkimer was mortally wounded.

Herkimer wasn't the first soldier to be ambushed by Indians, nor was Fetterman, mentioned earlier. Hollywood made the Indian ambush a stereotype in the movies, together with the brash headstrong leader. The oldest and dumbest of them was Henry Fonda ("Fort Apache"), who seemingly hadn't learned a thing in the hundred years since "Drums Along The Mohawk". As kids at the Saturday matinee we used to wonder how grown-ups could be so dumb as to not listen to John Wayne.

Anyway, guess who finally drove the British out of the Mohawk Valley? Benedict Arnold, in his patriotic days, and without firing a shot. But the NY State Historical Sign doesn't mention Arnold and I decided not to trust them after that. I trust no one who re-writes history.

I decided to exit the Thruway earlier than planned and saw a very large Beech Nut plant with a full parking lot as I reached Canajoharie. I wondered how much chewing gum they could make. Later I learned that the plant was making baby food.

Canajoharie means "washed pot" and the town has that name because a large circular "pot", washed out of stone by the waters of Canajoharie creek, lies within the town's limits. Susan B. Anthony, famous for her silver dollar, taught there for a while before moving on to become a suffragette, and George Washington slept there. When I first tried to research the town, I misspelled the name and got no hits on the Internet. I mistakenly concluded that little history had taken place in the town, very much like the house I once owned in Denver. It had a plaque I mounted that said, "On this site in 1876, nothing happened."

I drove parallel to the Mohawk River/Barge Canal, which were sometimes separate and sometimes the same body of water. Initially on the south bank, I crossed over at Glen and drove along the north bank to Amsterdam. I passed by Johnson Hall, 1749, the home of Sir William Johnson, a friend of the Indians for the British during The Seven Years War (French and Indian War as we called it), but didn't take the time to explore.

Amsterdam, NY is a rather large town, a city, actually, and is not to be confused with New Amsterdam, the original name of The Big Apple. There were a lot of good old brick buildings in town, and it seemed worthy of exploration, but as I climbed out of the Mohawk Valley, haunted by visions of Redcoats and Indian warriors, I saw the town's Wal-Mart, and I came back to reality. Eventually, I turned east, passed through Broadalbin (where did they get *that* name?) and spotted the blue peaks of the Adirondacks to the north.

I reached Saratoga Springs (Health, History, Horses) and chose not to make the seven-mile trip down to the Saratoga Battlefield, a decision I now regret. Saratoga Springs is the home of some warm mineral springs (Health), near the site of the Revolutionary War battle (History) and is the home of a major racetrack (Horses). A nice place to visit, but…

I crossed the Hudson River at Schuylerville, then saw some draft horses in a pasture that were big, really, really big. How big were they? Well, I've stood next to some of the Budweiser Clydesdales and these guys could have competed with them.

Going up the east side of the Hudson I reflected that I hadn't seen a flat field in a hundred miles. I noticed an apple orchard whose trees had been trained to send their branches up, then down, and the effect was to remind me of the Enchanted Forest of lions and tigers and bears, oh my! The apple trees had lost their leaves but not their apples, which only compounded the weird effect.

I reached Granville, NY, just this side of the Vermont state line from Poultney, VT, where my cousins live. Not wanting to be a burden for lunch, I stopped at a McDonald's and saw one of the employees take her lunch outside on what had turned out to be a beautiful sunny day. "Why," I asked myself, "Didn't I?"

There are several ways to get from Granville to Poultney, but I played it safe and followed a map route rather than stumble about looking for long forgotten byways. I crossed the state line and drove up to Poultney past Lake St. Catherine, as pretty a lake as you'll find in New England. It was gouged out of the surrounding rock by the glaciers lo, these many years ago.

My cousin Barb owns a "camp" on the lake; a small cabin on the west side that she says is now worth a quarter million. Now I happen to know that there aren't too many folk in Poultney with that kind of money and she confirmed my suspicion when I suggested that it must be city dwellers from New York who are buying places for money like that. Next thing you know, Poultney will have a Starbucks.

I pulled up into the farmyard and saw a deer hanging in one of the sheds. Barb's son, Brian, had gotten his Vermont buck and was now off in Maine, seeking another one. Before I had a chance to get a picture, the local butcher showed up and carted it off for slicing.

BARTLETT

I spent a few days with cousins Barb and Christine. Their mother had been the only one of my mother's siblings to remain in Vermont. There is a photograph, which I once copied and sent to all parties, of Barb and her brother Ted (Chris hadn't been born), and of me and my sister Peg, taken at my grandmother's farm in Poultney. It's dated July 4, 1944. This is remarkable in several aspects: first, we are all still alive after more than 60 years, and second, it was surprising to me that we had made it from Providence, RI to Poultney, VT, a distance of about 200 miles, during the War. We're talking a month after D-Day. Peggy told me the answer to that– my uncle Jack had taken us there. He had a car and had somehow managed the rationing coupons for gas and tires in order to make the trip there and back.

Well, that's how far back I go with Barb, my favorite cousin through all the years. Barb lost her husband to cancer in the 90s, so on top of everything, we have that in common as well.

Words cannot express the warm feelings I had of being in the bosom of family. We toured the Poultney area, went to Fair Haven, Granville and Hampton, the site of Quigley's Tavern, my father's favorite watering spot when he was in town. And we went to The Farm, as I think of it, the old homestead at Grandma's place, which was sold after she and her husband died.

There was a workman on the premises who told us that the owner had finally decided to fix the place up and live in it (it was built in 1873), and that he was anxious to talk to someone who knew the previous residents. Chris, the family historian, volunteered to get in touch. I later heard that Barb found out that the guy had been involved in a few shady deals and advised Chris to keep distant.

I noticed a sign that said Poultney had been chartered in 1761, and I have to confess that I knew very little of the town's history. Time for research. It seems that the Royal Governor of New Hampshire, Benning Wentworth, chartered many of Vermont's towns around that time. He granted (read: sold) patents to settlers in what was then called the Hampshire Grants. This land was later disputed by New York, whose borders had been changed from the Hudson to the Connecticut River by none other than that Consummate Villain, George III. Dispute over ownership and taxes led to the rise of Ethan Allen and The Green Mountain Boys, a group of thugs who terrorized New York tax collectors on behalf of the Hampshire men. The dispute was settled with the establishment of Vermont as a separate entity.

Wentworth wanted to curry favor awfully badly and saw to it that the towns were named for influential people in England. Except, of course for *Benning*ton, a tribute to his own ego. Lord William Poultney, the Earl of Bath got his immortality in Vermont. Ethan Allen got his at Fort Ticonderoga.

Horace Greeley, whose advice I followed (Go West, young man), apprenticed in Poultney, and George Jones, co-founder of the New York Times, was born and raised there. Green Mountain College, co-ed when founded in 1834, women-only in 1943 when the boys were off to war, and co-ed again in 1974, is the landmark at the end of Main Street. There are no fast food restaurants in Poultney, nor any restaurant where you can buy dinner. No hotels, either. But, as the central town in Slate Valley, Poultney gives good slate.

I left Poultney on a cloudy day damp with the prom-ise of rain; fortunately there was little prospect for snow, since it was too warm. I reached VT 4A at Castleton Corners, the location of a gas station where my father had once stopped for gas in the 50s. While there, I had picked up a pamphlet from the gasoline company that had sponsored the Washington Redskins professional football team. I hadn't even known there was such a thing as professional football, but I have been a Redskins fan ever since.

4A is the old road; a new VT 4 parallels it and is a high speed, 4-lane highway, the kind I like to avoid. The Olde Road goes through one of the classiest acts in Vermont, the town of Castleton, home of Castleton State College. The town is filled with stately old Colonial homes; I suppose the architecture is technically Georgian. They're all painted white, and I often wondered if there was a town ordinance requiring the color. The place is certainly a landmark. I took the time to drive onto the college campus and noticed that the newer buildings were brick, but they had white painted Georgian entrances. The library was named for Calvin Coolidge, a Vermonter.

President Coolidge was known to be a man of few words. I read somewhere that a Washington belle approached him and said, "Mr. President, my husband bet me that I couldn't get you to say three words." Calvin's response? "You lose." Of course.

I'm dwelling on this part of the journey because I was feeling quite nostalgic. When I was a kid and we made the long, long journey from Providence to Poultney, seven hours in those days, certain scenes became fixed in my mind and familiar landmarks were eagerly anticipated. Castleton, with its white houses, was one of them. So, too, were Chester, VT (stone houses), and a spring outside Ludlow, VT that sent water from a mountain through a pipe and into a large cauldron. We always stopped for a stretch and a drink at that spring and when my uncle Adam traveled with us, I always managed to find some change "someone" had dropped. I never really caught on to that until I was an adult, and the memory of my uncle "salting the mine" brings misty eyes for the lost innocence of those moments.

I drove on Route 4A alone for the first time ever and noticed that the road follows a valley, with a stream heading east towards Rutland and the inevitable railroad tracks alongside it. The grass was still green in Vermont; winter was taking its time getting there. Whether this was from the effects of Global Warming or from winter just taking its time getting there, no one could tell. Vermonters, being as I think they are, weren't going to worry about it, either.

Of note in the area was the Hubbardton Battlefield to the north, where a group of locals stood off the British in the only battle to be fought in Vermont during the Revolution. Farther south the Battle of Bennington was actually fought in New York. Both battles confounded General John Burgoyne on his way to Doom in Saratoga.

Also to the north is Proctor, site of a large marble quarry, opened at about the time the famous Carrara quarry in Italy became too deep to work. Michelangelo had shopped at Carrara, but lived too early to get to Proctor. Evidence of Proctor marble was in the faces of West Rutland's high school and town library.

How to tell the "haves" from the "have-nots" in Vermont: the haves put decorative shutters on their houses. My grandmother was a "have-not" in a financial sense; although her house had shutters, they were functional. Being a "have" doesn't mean you have taste, however, I saw a white house with crimson shutters next to a crimson barn with a tin roof and the overall effect was hideous. Must have been New Yorkers. City people.

Rutland, VT had always been a dingy town and still is. I drove through it quickly and began climbing up to Killington on the ridgeline of the Green Mountains. Susan and I had stayed in a dreadful B&B near there during our trip East, but we had a wonderful time anyway. Our life together was like that. We could make a feast out of beans on toast.

It was foggy as I reached the crest, near the Pico Mountain ski area, but there was no snow. A hunter stepped out of the woods, dressed in cammies, carrying a scoped rifle and wearing a bright orange vest. I'll say that again, cammies and a fluorescent orange vest. Ludicrous. Sure hope no one mistook him for a deer. (OK, later I found out that deer are colorblind, but it seems to me the vest must have disturbed the camouflage pattern to some degree, and again, if Carlin said it…)

As I made my way down the far side of the mountain I noticed the maximum speed in Vermont was 50 miles per hour and that was OK with me. Who'd want to go faster through one of the prettiest states in the Union? Well, all right, but not many Californians get out there.

I was now following a river downstream towards the Connecticut, but had no idea what its name was, many states post signs at river crossings, but Vermont doesn't. Forced to look at the map, I discovered I was following the Quechee, and I'm still not sure how to pronounce it.

In Bridgewater an old mill had been taken over for retail shops and I stopped there to browse. I recalled that Susan and I had done the same thing, and I found nothing of interest either visit. Further on in Woodstock (no, the rock concert was near Woodstock, NY) I recalled the general store that seemed to go on forever and saw again the pleasant and neat shops lining its main street. And here, as in Bridgewater I noticed the out-of-state plates were from Massachusetts instead of New York. So…that's how the bread in this part of Vermont gets buttered.

More observations on the road:

- It was Sunday and all the churches in Woodstock must have been having services at the same time, as there wasn't a parking place anywhere along the main street.

- A beautifully painted sign, gold letters on black background said, "Taftsville Burying Ground". Quaint.

- After passing a large covered bridge and a waterfall, I stopped at "Scotland by the Yard" and got a few items for my grandson, Cameron, with the Cameron clan tartan on them. (I have two grandsons, Camron belongs to Adam, my stepson, and Cameron is my son Michael's son.)

- In Quechee Lakes I saw Chester Arthur Road and that's the first time I ever saw something named for him.

- I crossed over Quechee Gorge and saw an antique mall that had proved disappointing on a previous trip. I didn't stop.

Crossing Vermont was an extremely peaceful journey; there were so many farms, so many trees, so many silos... I enjoyed the scenery despite a light drizzle and low overcast. I saw the Quechee join the White River, bypassed White River Junction and crossed a small stream that had to be the Connecticut River because without realizing it, I was suddenly in New Hampshire. No sign told me that, but all of the parked cars had NH plates (Live Free or Die).

For quite some distance I was tempted to give New Hampshire the same bad press I had once given Indiana. The towns certainly looked a bit more run-down than they had in Vermont. Very few houses were shuttered, lending credence to my "have-not" theory, and I saw virtually no farms. On the other hand, through my entire crossing of both states, I saw not one McDonalds or other fast-food chain place, so it wasn't all bad. One thing that was noticeable was that most of the trees were coniferous, a sign that I was perhaps in higher country; I couldn't tell because of the low overcast.

My high school chum, Jim, had told me that his town, Bartlett, was in the White Mountains, and as I swung north to get there, the towns took on a more prosperous appearance, thanks, no doubt, to tourism. Now, on NH 25 out of Meredith, it was downright pretty along the shores of Lake Winepasaukee. I had turned on the radio, tuned to a PBS station and found myself listening to old friend Garrison Keilor during his monologue about Lake Wobegon. It seemed most appropriate.

I made my way north, through Conway, a built up area of motels, shops and restaurants and saw signs warning of Moose Crossing. "Brake for Moose, It Could Save Your Life." Really? I passed a rest area with a scenic vista, but low hanging clouds socked everything in and I had no idea what made up the scenics. (In another Susan/Peter word play we pronounced that word "ske-nicks", and looked forward to them wherever advertised.)

Finally, I made it to Bartlett, found Jim's place with no trouble and was warmly welcomed by a friend I had not seen in 47 years. There are some men I hug and some men I don't hug, and I cannot tell you the difference. Jim and I came together instinctively in an embrace.

PROVIDENCE

The ground was thick with hoarfrost as I left Bartlett, NH early on a cold, crisp morning. I had risen with Jim and he was headed down to Concord for his two-day-a-week job and it seemed like the right thing to do to leave with him. His wife, Donna, had recently undergone minor surgery and was limited to her bed for a while; I look forward to spending more time with her some day.

They live in Donna's childhood home, a rambling house with attachments that were once a country store and a shed, heated by two woodstoves using six to seven cords of wood per year, certainly a picture of an idyllic New England life. Come to think of it, though, Jim never did tell me who chops the wood.

The visit with Jim shines as the most memorable one of the trip. Here were two 64-year-old men who hadn't seen one another since they were 17, who hadn't communicated much except to cite a few autobiographical facts and who took to each other as though no time had gone by at all. Despite all the clues in high school and before, I never quite realized what a gentle and sensitive being Jim was and what a wonderful man he would become. The best athlete of our triumvirate, he confessed that he'd actually been shy in school and had made some life and career choices to overcome that shyness. I had never guessed.

The "triumvirate" I refer to consisted of Jim, myself, and Richard, the fellow I was to see in Providence. Jim and I wasted no time in describing our lives to one another, good and bad. It seemed as though we were in school again, confessing confidences that would go no further, and unashamedly describing faults and errors in our respective lives; faults and errors that made no difference to our friendship. We'd shared our hopes and dreams in high school and now, as men, we were sharing our realities.

A more intimate conversation was not to be had on my entire trip. I couldn't put my finger on it at the time – I still have difficulty putting it into words – but the absolute *comfort* I felt in Jim's presence, despite the years that had gone by, settled on me like a well-worn blanket. I had driven over 4,000 miles to Bartlett, I had to leave much too soon, but I am damn glad I made the trip.

Bartlett was named for Josiah Bartlett who, as we all know, was the guy who signed the Declaration of Independence right below John Hancock. Well, we know it now, don't we? I didn't get much of a chance to see the town, as I arrived in the late afternoon and left in the early morning next day. This was one of those time-compressed visits I made because of my need to be in Delaware for Thanksgiving.

For the first time in my journey I retraced my steps as I sped southward through New Hampshire bound for Massachusetts and then, Providence, RI. In Conway, NH I encountered heavy traffic and discovered it was due to a high school crossing. Leave it to me to notice a very pretty young blonde in a pink exercise outfit, a gorgeous girl walking all alone, and I wondered if none of the boys had the courage to approach her, or if she were simply unapproachable. Had I been a teen at her school, I would have been mortified, unable to speak to her. Jim hadn't been the only shy one.

Outside of Conway, I saw the dreaded moose warning sign, this one for 17 miles of crossings. I had learned from Jim, and later from an article in New England Magazine, that the threat of moose collision was very real, particularly during the autumn rutting season. Seems the males get infatuated with the musk in the air and tend to lose their heads, cross the roads ignoring all traffic, or simply stand there and invite doom. I've known some men to do the same sort of thing.

Mind you, a moose has much longer legs than deer or elk, and that means that the body of the critter is what comes directly through your windshield. So, Beware of Moose. They kill people.

The day turned from a high overcast to bright sunshine and I was comfortable to be in New England, where distances are short and speed limits are low and all's right with the world. Glacial boulders were everywhere in New Hampshire and stone walls and stone foundations were commonplace. Back in North Conway I had passed through a commercial strip, a New England commercial strip, with business signs tastefully done, very little neon and good looking colonial architecture. It was quite different from the same kind of strip I'd seen elsewhere in the country. There was a 1768 Country Inn with in-room fireplaces, and I thought, "Sure, just like in Southern California." Sure.

Other observations in New Hampshire:

- Dirty Works Greenhouse and Nursery was NOT on Potting Bench Road.

- A shop was called Piccalilly and I remembered a substance, a kind of relish we put on hot dogs when I was a kid and I was sure it was called piccalilli.

- Lickety-Split Ice Cream, make your own sundaes.

- The New Hampshire license plate has the state motto: Live Free or Die. Exemplified by the state law: Buckle up under age 18. Upon reaching majority, you can live free and die.

- And finally, in the last rest area before entering Massachusetts, there is a state liquor store that also sells lottery tickets. Only time I have ever seen a liquor store in a rest area.

Soon, I was on Interstate highway, again because I was pressed for time. I had called Richard and found that he had forgotten about a class he had to attend that evening down in Newport. It appeared that I'd have only a few hours with him and then be moving on towards my sister's house in Delaware. This was to be the only schedule glitch in my entire journey.

In Massachusetts I got onto I-95, which I believed I'd be seeing a lot of in the next few weeks, as it goes completely down the Eastern Seaboard. I discovered that it bypassed Boston and ran in the roadbed of what used to be MA 128, the beltway that had grown a lot of high tech businesses. I found out later that another Interstate went to Boston and went through a tunnel under the city, known as The Big Dig, which had encountered problem after problem and still leaked. I'm glad I missed it.

I passed Lexington and Concord, bowed my head in the direction of those shrines, and tuned the radio to WGBH, the famous Boston Public Radio station. I passed Newton, where Richard, I, and a few others had gone for a high school math contest and I discovered that I was no mathematician. This didn't deter me from entering Brown later to study *Applied* Mathematics.

As I commented to myself that the woods in New England seem so very thick I suddenly found myself in Rhode Island. I was "home" for the first time since Dad died in 1986.

I was born in Providence in 1940, a second generation American. All of my grandparents immigrated to America from Poland in the early 1900s, although it wasn't called that at the time. Poland did not officially come back into existence until after World War I.

My mother's parents, the Polesiaks, established themselves on a farm in the small hamlet of West Pawlet, Vermont. My father's folks settled in Providence, Rhode Island, where my mother and most of her siblings came to seek work in the 1920s.

We lived on the ground floor of a three-tenement house in a two-bedroom place without hot water or central heating. The kitchen stove in winter heated our "house" and we generally closed off the "parlor" to conserve heat. Our kitchen stove was fired by coal during WWII and converted to oil thereafter. When I was a toddler, the biggest threat my parents held over me for obedience was to be sent away with the coalman, a creature who carried sacks of coal from a truck at the curb and poured it down a chute into our basement. He was, of course, blackened with coal dust, and very frightening. I must have been relieved when our stove was converted to burn oil.

My earliest memories are from pre-school days. I remember VE Day, which I think was May 8, 1945. I was a few days short of five years old and was riding a tricycle, which may or may not have been an early birthday present. Everybody had a flag and was waving and yelling except that it's very difficult for a five-year-old to clutch a flag and steer a tricycle at the same time, so it was no wonder that some "big guys" came along, questioned my patriotism ("Where's your flag, Runt?") and shoved me and my trike over on our sides. I went inside crying and learned two lessons: to have the utmost respect for the flag, and to be wary of "big guys". I still get a shiver down my spine when they play the National Anthem, and I own a 9mm pistol in case someone wants to shove me around.

Life in the winter centered around two objects in Chez Siedzick – that kitchen stove, bringer of warmth and food, and the radio, sole source of our entertainment. When we closed the parlor in the winter, Dad dragged the two easy chairs into the kitchen and created a sitting area around the table holding the radio. Those were the days, by the way, when you turned on the radio 2 or 3 minutes before your favorite program to give the tubes ample time to warm up. Same for early TV when it came along. Say the words, "tube tester" at your local hardware store nowadays and see what reaction you get.

Listening to the radio today means listening to music, shock jocks, news…mostly music. We listened to music then, too, but seldom at night. Nighttime was story time, and we were left with only words coming over the radio and our imaginations to fill in the blanks. I was able to create my own Lone Ranger Silver Mine, Jack Benny Vault and vampire bats from the Amazon jungle. You can watch Garrison Keilor on PBS sometime and perhaps see the guys who make the sound effects for his show, Prairie Home Companion. Take the mystery out of it, they do. Millions of people got shivers over the creaking door of "Inner Sanctum", without ever seeing it.

When I got old enough to go out at night, The Boys' Club kept me off the streets. And that was a good thing. In those days, the neighborhood was mostly an Italian one, and in Providence that meant that sooner or later someone would make a connection with the Mafia, the Family That Doesn't Exist. My father used to play the numbers at the local bars and I know that several of the kids I grew up with eventually made it into the Organization, so *something* existed. Those same kids were graduating into stealing hubcaps from cars at about the time I moved to another part of town.

That move, and the Boys' Club kept me from being tempted down their path. For years, when I worked and was "encouraged" to donate to the United Way, I used their elective card to see that my money went to the Boys' Club. When they withdrew their elective card, I withdrew my donations.

Now I was back in Providence and I exited the freeway and drove through Federal Hill, a section of Providence that had been predominantly Italian and now was home to at least one taco stand. Olneyville Square was still a traffic bottleneck and old McCaffrey's Drug Store had been turned into a Century 21.

McCaffery's was where we used to get coffee "cabinets", a milkshake made with coffee ice cream. Elsewhere, they are known as milkshakes, frappes or whatever trendy name might be popular, but in Providence they were cabinets, and I have never heard that name outside of town.

While I noticed the changes to the Square, I also saw that there was still a New York Hot System hot dog place. My father had taken me to one, across the street from the present location, when I was in 6th grade, ordered two hot dogs for me and only one for himself. That, I guess, was the Polish Catholic version of the bar mitzvah; at any rate, I felt pretty grown up.

I found Richard's home with no problem and found Richard to be the same busyholic he had been in school. A perpetual student, he was now studying for a degree in Holistic Counseling. Retired from being a Navy civilian, Richard had earned his Ph.D. in Electronics at Brown and, just as in high school, seemed to have his plate overflowing with "stuff". Richard and I did not hug.

We had lunch at an Indian restaurant on College Hill and walked down to tour the downtown area of Providence; it was much changed since I lived there. Then we went back up the hill to tour the Brown campus, where I had studied for a year before my Academy nomination came through. I became quite nostalgic on The Green, found the poolroom in the same location in the student union, and almost expected to find the same guy in charge, the one who had constantly cautioned me to "keep a firm bridge". I picked up a copy of The Brown Daily Herald and noted that nothing in student life seemed to have changed, at least on the fundamental levels.

Along the way, Richard and I talked of other times. We had been in the same classes in elementary school for as long as we could remember. We spoke of girls we'd had crushes on, or who had made moves on us (in the 6th grade!) and remembered names neither of us had spoken for decades. We talked about classmates who were successful and some who were obscure, some who had been cut short of life by dreaded disease or accidents and some who were still in Providence. Too quickly, it was time for Richard to head for Newport and for me to continue my journey.

During our walk in Providence Richard and I had our picture taken, a couple of bearded old gents totally unrecognizable from the photos in our yearbook. We both have half-smiles, but I can't help but feel there is something winsome in our looks, as though we longed for a chance to go back and do some of it over. Perhaps we did.

I cannot conceive of two men who could be more un-alike than Jim and Richard. And I am different from both. Yet we had been friends in school and are still friends. Their homes, like mine, are full of books, and each of us has had at least one failed marriage.

But those are biographical facts, not emotional issues. Each of us, it seemed, could not wait to tell the others about all the hang-ups we'd had in school and how we'd dealt with them and then went on to develop different hang-ups in adult life. And we'd dealt with those, as well. I had looked forward to the meetings without any expectations, content to observe and let my friends be whatever they had become. It turned out that they, like me, had become men the hard way. One day at a time, through trial and error, with success and failings, through joy and sadness. It shows in our faces, but not in our spirits. When I left Providence, at about the same time in the afternoon as I had arrived in Bartlett the previous day, I concluded that the 24 hours had been among the most moving of my life.

The picture of Richard and me was taken at about the point where the Providence River enters Narragansett Bay and I marked this as the official close of Episode I, "From Sea to Shining Sea" in my adventures. Now, as I left town I was embarking southbound on Episode II, which I thought I'd name "Whistling Dixie on the Molar Express", in honor of all the munchies I kept in the car, and the newly released movie, "Polar Express", which I hadn't yet seen.

At some point in Rhode Island I turned west for the first time in the trip, and realized that I was done with "Eastbound and down". Henceforth, while I would not be heading towards home, I would not be heading away from it anymore, either.

For now, though, I had to contend with traffic on I-95, on what used to be the Connecticut Turnpike, and I did so until I reached New Haven in the dark, and the less said about that leg, the better.

PART TWO
WHISTLIN' DIXIE ON THE MOLAR EXPRESS

WILLIAMSBURG

After a truly uneventful and forgettable night in New Haven, I left for Delaware. I had a reservation for a room in Dover, DE for one more night of solitude before six more nights of guesting.

I was, for all practical purposes, back in the New York Metro traffic I had abhorred for four years in the 70s and escaped via Denver. (Of course, I ended up spending 14 years in L.A. traffic, victim of The Revenge of The Traffic Gods). Once again, I thought of the bad rap I had given L.A. drivers and mumbled an apology – a small one, but an apology nevertheless. Metro drivers will be metro drivers, and I used to be one of them.

There is no gloom like New England gloom. I was affected by it and by the fact that I now was a little off schedule. I could go straight to my sister's house in one day, but I already was planning on a rather long visit there and didn't want to overstay my welcome. On the other hand, it was beginning to get uncomfortable to be alone for long periods. At times, I felt like I could have stayed in Bandon and grieved there.

And, I had been profoundly moved by my meetings with classmates from so long ago, and staying in a busy house, albeit with family, would detract from the time I needed for absorption of the experiences. I wanted to think, and I didn't need distractions, so I was intent to just get to Dover, and took Interstate highways all the way. Besides, this was very familiar ground.

I started west and saw a large bridge crossing the Housatonic River; it was probably on US 1, the old Boston Post Road. I recalled that my Dad used to take exits from the Connecticut Turnpike onto US 1 to avoid the tollbooths, and then get back on after he'd passed them. My mother, who did not drive, used to complain about the extra travel but, hey, back then a quarter was ¼ of a dollar and bought a pack of cigarettes.

The Connecticut Turnpike, I-95, is the only toll road I know of that has dismantled its tollbooths and stopped charging. I guess the original construction bonds have been paid off, but that's probably true of other toll roads as well, and, to the bureaucratic and political minds in many states, a cash cow is a cash cow.

In 2000, Susan and I came East for her first visit ever to New England. It was early autumn, greenery abounded in the neat villages we passed through and while she was driving along US 1 in Connecticut, I asked her what she thought of everything. She replied, "If I weren't driving on the wrong side of the road, I'd swear I was at home." Later, at lunch, she was amazed to discover fish and chips prepared in the English tradition, less the newspaper, of course. "There's more than one reason it's called New England," I told her. It was a warming experience to watch Susan, almost childlike in her wonder at the similarity of New England to her home. I got the feeling that she finally understood how I shared her disdain for the hedonism of Southern California.

On that trip she saw many town names that had originated in England, and were duplicated in several New England states. She was surprised to discover Manchester in New Hampshire, Vermont and Connecticut. There's an area of Providence known as Manchester, too, but it's not incorporated as such.

Passing through Bridgeport, CT, I noted that there is quite a bit of difference between the views from it, and Bridgeport, CA. The former is, and always has been, an industrial city with a pretty ugly skyline; the latter sits at 6,000 feet elevation and commands an outstanding view of the snowy granite peaks of the Sierra Nevada. Nevertheless, historically at least, the Connecticut city has the edge. Saved from burning by Admiral Lord Howe during the Revolution, the city actually erected a statute to him in a park and the favorite line there was, "Would you like to go to Seaside Park and see Howe standing up behind a bench?"

There were still quite a few golden leaves on the trees in Connecticut; it wasn't as stark as in New Hampshire. As the clouds began to break a little, I managed to see a patch of sunshine strike Long Island Sound, grunted, "Sea to Shining Sea, indeed," and put my nose in the direction of the long ribbon of macadam that would take me south, at last whistling "Dixie", but alas, with no munchies in the car to make it the Molar Express.

And how many trips did we make with this kind of dialogue:

"Susan, did we bring any goodies to munch on?" I asked.

"No, Peter, we didn't," she replied.

"Then I shall have to suffer," I said, waiting for her to join me in the chorus, "BUT NOT IN SILENCE."

I briefly considered going down into The City, crossing the George Washington Bridge and getting into New Jersey that way, but P.D. said, "No, stick with the plan," and so I crossed Westchester County, scene of my first marriage, and approached the Tappan Zee Bridge over the Hudson. Seems the local Indian tribe were the Tappans and the first settlers, who were Dutch of course, called this wider expanse of the Hudson a "zee", just like Holland's Zuider Zee that we all learned about in grade school.

The river is about three miles wide here and from the height of the span I could see some of the New York skyline and one tower of the GW Bridge. So I bypassed New York City. Don't get me wrong, I love the place, there is vibrancy in the streets of Manhattan unmatched by any other city I've been in. I just hate getting into and out of it.

I've harped about America from the Interstate, but America from the Garden State Parkway is an exception. Parkway, of course, is the term we use for "NO TRUCKS", and besides allowing for a gentler drive without having to dodge the Kings of the Road, the scenery is a lot prettier. I passed many a suburban tract with well-kept homes, nice landscaping and trees of many colors. At one point a deer with a wonderful rack ran out to the road, thought better of jumping the guard rail and turned around into someone's back yard. All these miles and the first *live* deer I see is on the Parkway in New Jersey! Go figure.

The farther south I went the more leaves I saw on trees; there was a weeping willow, still green on top and yellow on the bottom. A truck belonging to a contractor with the same name as the guy whom I used in Bandon passed me. He had kept us in a vacation rental for seven weeks while completing the job he estimated to take only two. I thumbed my nose. I dared not use a stronger signal; after all, I was in New Jersey.

Then it was time to make the transition from the Garden State Parkway to the New Jersey Turnpike and the less said about that transition and the Turnpike, the better. Trucks again.

I crossed the Delaware Memorial Bridge into Delaware; traffic on the turnpike had been surprisingly light for the day before the day before a major holiday, and I was grateful. I drove over the Chesapeake and Delaware Canal, completed in 1829, once a lock canal until bought by the US Army Corps of Engineers and converted to a sea-level thoroughfare.

I arrived in the Dover area too early for check-in, so I had a late lunch, toured a local mall, where I bought a Peter, Paul and Mary tape (yes, tape, I don't have a CD player in the big car) and visited a Wal-Mart for some herbal supplements. This was the third Wal-Mart I'd entered that was substandard in comparison to the ones I'd shopped in Nevada and Oregon. The aisles were narrow and crammed with merchandise and there was an overall dingy effect. Moreover, the employees back home seemed always cheerful and willing to help, not the case in the East. No wonder the company gets a lot of bad press.

I stopped in a lot of Wal-Mart's on this trip, because I knew they would have what I wanted, and in most instances I was greeted by an old-timer who needed the work for one reason or another and who seemed glad to have the job. I don't know where those folks could have gone for a job otherwise.

Next morning I started out on the short drive to my sister Peg's house, intending to stop at antique stores along the way, only to discover that there weren't any. "OK," I thought, "I'll save myself for the big one in Millsboro." I passed Dover AFB on my left and saw some BIG Air Force transports, and noted the temperature was 56 degrees. It hadn't been that warm since I was in Nebraska, the day it was in the 60s, and how many days ago had that been, I wondered?

Delaware is flat, really flat. I drove past green fields with short growth alternating with crops as yet un-harvested, all carefully husbanded. At one point I saw a sign for Delaware Bay fishing, on Head Boats or Charter Boats. The term "Head Boat" intrigued me, and I just KNEW that it didn't mean what I wished it meant. Subsequent research on the Internet led to many, many sites offering the services of

Head Boats, but none defined the term for me. I remain mystified.

After my coast-to-coast trip to be there at Thanksgiving, I almost expected to hear a fanfare of trumpets when I arrived. Alas, it was not to be. Peggy, with some of her New England upbringing showing, said, "Hi." We were never ones to embrace, though I often hug rather than shake hands, and on this occasion we did neither. It wasn't a disappointment to me; it's just the way we are.

I suppose some analysts could make a big deal out of that; nowadays, everybody seems to watch Dr. Phil or someone like him. Most people my age, though, seem to accept "it's just the way we are" without further explanation.

I did get a big hug from Carolyn, Peggy's younger daughter. Developmentally disabled since birth, Carolyn exhibits that kind of unconditional love that we all talk about, but are seldom able to give.

Everyone had a fine time at my sister's house for a combined Thanksgiving/Birthday celebration. Peg was born on November 29th and whenever the 29th falls on a Thursday, it is the fifth Thursday of the month, a week after Thanksgiving. Sort of like the people born on February 29th.

Peggy's older daughter, Cathy and her husband, Randy, arrived with their daughter, Jessica. Jessie was a freshman at the local community college where she, like so many others, was trying to decide what to do with the rest of her life. When we played a few card games during the weekend, I could see Jessie's internal struggle between the woman she wanted to be and the girl she still was.

Cathy's son, Michael, was too busy to make the trip. Also a college student, he runs a part-time lawn business, plays hockey and, I think, spends a lot of time fighting off girls. He's a good-looking kid.

It was an emotional departure for me, though, as Joe, Peggy's husband is suffering from the dementia that plagued his mother, and it's sad that Peggy has to watch the slow deterioration of the mind, if not the body and the spirit. I think that's worse than my experience with Susan, so I feel my sister's pain very deeply.

My destination was Williamsburg, VA and the home of Sam and Kay. Sam was my best man in my first marriage, and was married to Kay at Fort Bragg, where my first wife and I played host to Kay before the wedding. I'd not seen them in decades.

My route took me the length of the Delmarva Peninsula, a long flat journey bordered by green fields and dense forests. I reflected on how my sister had managed to get me and her family out to shop on Black Friday, to a mall in Salisbury, MD. I NEVER go shopping on days after holidays when the stores are jammed, but it seems to be a family tradition for them. I did enjoy shopping the aforementioned antique store later and, as usual, came away with a few old books, published prior to 1900.

After stopping in Pokemoke City, MD, for gas and food, the weather closed in around me; it became foggy, misty, with low visibility. It was dismal. I put my nose to the grindstone and noted that it was 103 miles to Norfolk, then a short drive up to Williamsburg where I'd be a guest again – wow! What a great title – A Guest Again!

Right after I crossed the Virginia state line, I noticed that gas was a lot cheaper than in Maryland. But I'd contributed to Maryland's tax coffers and it was too late to economize. In Temperance, VA, I passed a Tyson chicken processing plant and the smell was awful. I hadn't thought about it, but I suppose they're processing a lot of chicken guts… Later I drove by a Perdue plant and the odor wasn't noticeable; maybe it was the wind direction.

The clouds began to break up as I approached the Chesapeake Bay Bridge-Tunnel and by the time I got onto the bridge itself, I was in full sunshine. With Chesapeake

Bay on my right and the Atlantic Ocean on my left, I paid my 12 dollar toll and enjoyed the sight of ocean-going vessels lined up in Hampton Roads, fishermen plying back and forth along the pylons of the bridge and, as I approached the south end, homes along the beach with people fishing in the surf.

I reached Virginia Beach and saw a sign for Pleasure House Road, and was mightily tempted, but yea, I take my daily vitamins and have the strength of ten. So I drove on.

After crossing the James River via another bridge/tunnel combination, I drove up I-64 and saw the sign, "Speed Limit Enforced by Aircraft," and wondered how they did that. Do they land on top of your car and write a ticket? Maybe "Speed Limit <u>Observed</u> by Aircraft" is a better way of putting it?

If it seems that I'm a pain in the ass about proper English, I am. I had a proper English wife, for one thing, and I was a professional salesman for decades, for another. Communication, I learned, is not that easy unless words are carefully chosen. When I hear teens, or worse, adults, say, "Like, you know..." I want to shake them and say, "No, I don't know, spell it out for me." Unfortunately, they're very often incapable of doing so, and blame *me* for not under-standing. End of tirade.

I passed a sign for Yorktown and remembered that, thirty years before, when our family had visited Williams-burg and Jamestown, we hadn't driven to Yorktown. Since then I've become a voracious reader on the Revolution; I had to see the battlefield and made a note to ask Sam to include it on our tour.

I got lost trying to follow Sam's directions, called their house on the cell phone and got straightened out. Who was it that said, "I've never been permanently lost?"

PINEHURST

I simply did not spend enough time with Sam and Kay. Sam was thoughtful enough to take a few days off work to be my splendid host and I appreciated that beyond words. He is a Government Contractor to the Department of Defense, and rather than have him say, "If I tell you what I do, I'll have to kill you," I let it go at that. We crammed in a lot of touring in the area and never really had the chance to sit and gab about new and old times. OK, next visit.

Asked about my preferences for touring, I immediately responded with "Yorktown". We got onto the Williamsburg-Yorktown Parkway, a National Historic District in itself and went over to the town and the battlefield.

I love reading about the Revolution. It's the defining point, or maybe I should say process, of our country and where the ideals and principles of America were put into print, in some cases in granite. I often wonder what the Founding Fathers would think of America today. I have my own interpretation of the Constitution and it often differs radically from the Court's more liberal opinions.

The first thing that strikes me about any Colonial era fort or battlefield is size. When I was trained as an Infantry officer in the 1960s, I was expected to defend a platoon front of 300-500 yards with the 40 or so men in my unit. But they were armed with automatic and semi-automatic weapons, and the limited firepower of the 1700s soldier meant that that same area would have to be defended by several thousand men, standing three deep and shoulder-to shoulder. The Yorktown Battlefield is small.

I had seen maps of Yorktown in many books, but none of them ever detailed the marsh and swamp of the Yorktown River to the west and north of town. They only left those areas blank and showed the American and French siege lines mostly in the south. Now I saw how difficult it would have been for either side to sally in that area. What I really wanted to see were the redoubts, numbered 9 and 10, which the British had pushed out ahead of their lines and whose loss forced the capitulation. Redoubt 10 was taken by a night bayonet charge led by Lt. Col Alexander Hamilton, whose fate it was to be later downed by a single shot from Aaron Burr.

Cornwallis came out on the short end of the Battle of Yorktown, but I think few Americans realize that he went on to a distinguished career, including being named Viceroy of India, a colony the British were able to hang onto for another 150 years. All my studies of the Revolution and of Yorktown convince me that Cornwallis almost wanted to lose; that he saw the war as an immense drain on England's resources and maybe even foresaw the partnership that has endured for several centuries. On the other hand, maybe he just blundered by getting bottled up in Yorktown, unusual for a British general, what?

The town of Yorktown itself is small. I wondered where the hell they quartered the 7,000 British troops and ancillaries back then. Most of the town looked to me pretty much as it must have in 1781. Other than taking some family pictures at Thanksgiving, this was the first time I used my camera on the trip. It came out again in Williamsburg and later in San Antonio.

Sam and I avoided the touristy area of Jamestown, where a model of the Susan Constant is anchored, and opted for the historical site, consisting largely of foundations in the ground and statues of John Smith and Pocahontas. It was of interest to see the archaeological dig and the cleaning and sorting of artifacts. I wouldn't have the patience to deal with that sort of thing. Sam bought a hat at the shop there and it led to a discussion on follicle challenge, but the storekeeper, who was really behaving like a witch there in Jamestown, wasn't buying into our play and folderol, so we decided to call her That Witch in Jamestown, and left.

We were having lunch at a pleasant café in Williamsburg, close to the College of William and Mary, when a well-groomed blonde lady in her 40s strode in with a splendidly manicured hand incongruously scratching her ass all the way from the front door to the ladies room, and then exited without buying anything. "Must be a regular," I thought, one with an itchy stretch girdle.

As we walked around the campus, I shot more pictures, intending to send some to Mary Ellen, back in Denver, who had attended William and Mary before her roots snapped her back to Texas. We were overtaken at one point by a young couple striding purposefully along hand-in-hand and discussing, of all things, the merits of PowerPoint6. Did we talk about such things when I was in college? To girls, I mean? While holding hands?

Sam and I took a walk from the campus down Duke of Gloucester Street to the Capitol, noting the fine buildings, chatting about whatnot and taking pictures here and there, including one of the blonde from the café. She wasn't my type, really, but I wanted to document her coiffure. The area was largely deserted, due to the fact that Colonial Williamsburg is falling on hard times and many of the exhibits have been cut back.

Dinner that night was at Shields' Tavern, partaking of "Mr. Shields' Bountiful Feast": all you could eat of corn chowder, ribs, chicken, vegetables and other fare that I found far too bland for my taste. Entertainment was provided by various players in Colonial costume and was more than compensation for the food.

All too soon it was time to leave for Pinehurst, NC to meet with my cousin Ted, Barb's brother, who was visiting his son there. I left Williamsburg, passing the entrance to Camp Peary, which, I think, is the training "Farm" of the CIA. I really didn't have a feel for how long the trip would take, I had learned to distrust estimates I got on the Internet, and so I started out on Interstates again to make some time. Up to Richmond and then southbound and down on I-295 leading to good ol' I-95.

Back in the old days, when I traveled from New York down to Fayetteville, NC, we used US 1 through Virginia and rode the roller coaster up and down across all the stream channels that run east-west. The Interstates have pretty much flattened out the drive. To relieve the monotony there were plenty of dead critters, even a deer, along the road, but I didn't keep a head count.

The "old days" I refer to are the early 60s, shortly after graduation and commissioning, when I was assigned to Ft Benning, GA for training and Fort Bragg, NC for duty with the 82d Airborne. With my wife's mother in New York and my parents in New England, it meant we made a lot of trips up and down the East Coast, and during that time saw a great many changes in the highway system.

I realized that finally I was going in the right direction, meaning that the mile markers going southbound and, later, westbound, would be counting down to the next state line. I wondered how many re-surfacings the road had had since I first traveled it in the 60s. Back then, one had to use US 301 for the sections of the Interstate that hadn't opened yet. I may have finally driven all the way on I-95 only after reassignment to Panama in '65, and during a final road trip down to Charleston, SC for embarkation.

Outside of Skippers, VA I saw a sign for Dry Bread Road. Begs the question, doesn't it? In North Carolina I-95 became the Purple Heart Memorial Highway. When I stopped at a rest area and checked a map, I discovered I would get to Pinehurst much too early for my hotel so I decided to get off the Interstate and meander. With that, I started on the last bottle from the six-pack of water I had bought all the way back in Brush, CO. Or was it Fort Morgan?

Westbound on NC 42 I saw a sign for Rock Ridge, and here I thought they invented that name for the movie "Blazing Saddles". After nothing but scrub oak and pine forests along the Interstate it was nice to pass through farms - farms that were well taken care of and had shutters on the farmhouses. (There were shutters on the houses in Colonial Williamsburg, but it was easy to see that they were solid and functional, not louvered and decorative.)

Suddenly, a herd of four deer began running across the wide expanse of lawn at the Thanksgiving Baptist Church, headed right at the road. As I began to brake, they turned and ran back, saving me from eating a deer in the windshield and causing me to give thanksgiving. I had actually thought at first that they were big dogs.

Random thoughts as I crossed North Carolina:

- I don't know how to pronounce Fuquay Varina, a town I passed.

- Duncan, NC is the home of Duncan Junction, a convenience store.

- For some reason, North Carolina posts signs indicating what river basin you're passing into. I don't know why they think this is important to people.

- Corinth, NC had Christmas decorations out, including a Nativity scene on public land.

- I saw some cattle, each with a massive white stripe around the middle of their bodies. The rest of the cow was black. I don't know the name of the breed.

- Every time I topped a hill I saw...another pine covered hill.

And so it went until I reached Pinehurst, did a mall crawl until check-in time, hooked up with Ted and his wife, Kay and met his family, ate dinner, talked a lot, and so to bed.

TUSCALOOSA

When I was a kid, both my sister and my cousin Ted were five or more years older than I, a gulf that seemed then to be wider than I could ever leap. Today, in retirement, we all seem to have a lot more in common than we ever did as kids, and I don't mean just in memories.

Ted used to be the high school football coach in a small upstate New York town. Some of his players not only went to college on scholarship, but a few, I believe, made it to the Pros. His infectious and abounding enthusiasm and optimism are still alive at 70. Quite a guy.

I left Pinehurst on a misty, rainy day, with low, scudding clouds, but the Weather Channel had assured me that I would eventually be in sunshine on my way to Georgia. Pinehurst oozes affluence. All the buildings were brick and I doubt that any resident had less than a half-acre of land. After negotiating a traffic circle with five, count 'em five, major signed highways radiating in and out and creating unbelievable congestion, I traveled west on NC 211 towards Candor. I passed an Upscale Retail store in the Camellia Park Shops and noted that, since Park wasn't spelled "Parke", it couldn't have been too exclusive.

I reached and passed the village of Candor and wondered if the residents practiced it; I didn't stop to find out. I was well aware from a previous trip of what the residents practiced in Intercourse, PA.

As I drove under low, dark, threatening clouds, I could see a line of blue on the horizon and knew that I'd reach sunshine in less than an hour. In Bisco, NC, just after the Bisco Police Department, I saw a post office and remembered that I had to buy and mail a condolence card to my neighbor, Jean. Jean's husband, Bill, a graduate of the

Naval Academy, had passed away during Thanksgiving week and, as I had heard she wasn't taking calls, I figured I'd better get a card to her. The ever-present Wal-Mart on the edge of town supplied me with one.

Bill had been a New Englander, like myself, and had graduated from the Academy in 1949. He went into Naval Aviation and had flown prop-driven planes off of aircraft carriers, though he hadn't seen service in Korea. Whenever we got together, the good-natured banter included remarks about "ground-pounders" and questions about the flight characteristics of the Sopwith Camel.

But Bill had been ill for a long time with a variety of ailments and when his organs began to shut down he was hospitalized. The female minister of his church went by to deliver a final blessing and got rather emotional, so Bill, a lay reader at St. John's, took the prayer book and read his own last rites. He was a take-charge guy to the end, and he will be sorely missed.

The drive across North Carolina to Pinehurst had seemed idyllic the day before; now I was aiming for a stopover point near Atlanta and I felt as though the pressures of "getting there" were on me. It got worse, as we'll see. The route through the western parts of North and South Carolina and north Georgia was through pine forest. Everywhere. Was this what I came East for?

In one small town I had been following a truck towing a trailer full of wooly-looking pigs and just before it turned off to the left, I noticed a deer writhing on the ground beside the road. The deer had obviously been struck by a vehicle and was in its death throes. The pigs were probably on their way to becoming bacon, and I wondered why the farmer hadn't stopped to count coup on the deer. After all, he could have added venison to the menu, if the butcher knew anything about deer.

My tape through this leg of the trip became little more than grunted observations. Either I hadn't slept well and was tiring, or I was just getting tired of driving.

Someone had taken over a motel and put up a temporary sign, "Exeuctive Inn", and stood waiting for the "exeuctive" world to beat a path to his door. Albemarle, NC, a classy sounding town had every chain store and fast food restaurant in America along its main street, with attendant signage disguising whatever charm it might possess. I crossed Little Long Creek and looked for the inevitable and found it – Long Creek. Obviously, I was getting bored.

I reached the Interstate, I-85, and immediately became disgusted with the truck traffic. In most states there are lane restrictions for trucks and when there aren't, most truck drivers are courteous enough to get back into the right lane after passing. Not so in South Carolina and Georgia. Truckers were driving wherever they wanted, at whatever speeds they wanted and the passenger car be damned. I had never seen such undisciplined truck traffic, not even in Mexico. I must have missed, by the way, the day in kindergarten when we were taught, "Mr. Trucker Is Our Friend." He sure wasn't on this leg of the trip.

In South Carolina I crossed the Broad River, which wasn't. Gaffney, SC had a water tower tank painted, and in the shape of, a peach, and I wondered why. I drove 106 miles of South Carolina Interstate highway and it is nearly all best forgotten.

Upon entering Georgia, I noticed that their "Buckle Up" sign was a red field in the shape of the state, with blue belts and white buckles to give an overall effect, or illusion, of the Confederate battle flag. In all my travels I saw but one Confederate flag flying, in a private yard beneath a U.S. flag. I know there's been a lot of hullabaloo about the Confederate flag and my own opinion is that it doesn't represent slavery. A lot of Southerners who never owned a slave fought under that flag.

People should be allowed to fly any flag they want as long as it doesn't fly higher than the Stars and Stripes. Well, swastikas might not be a good idea. Personally, I would like to fly the Jolly Roger, as I am much into pillage. Watch me at garage sales and flea markets.

And while on the subject of States' Rights, I had become quite disappointed in this southbound leg of the journey as I had consumed very few munchies, after noting that my weight had climbed ten pounds, and "Whistlin' Dixie on the Molar Express" hadn't been a totally accurate motto. Nevertheless, the phrase is catchy, and I'll hold onto it, lack of molarization notwithstanding.

I passed a sign for the Admiral Benbow Inn and it struck a chord; wasn't that the name of the inn in "Treasure Island"? Yup, but who was Admiral Benbow? A brave fellow, in fact, who gave chase to a larger enemy squadron, and was mortally wounded before seeing justice done to the cowardly captains who refused to follow him. But that was before my time, in 1702.

I reached the Atlanta area, took the beltway around the city, and finally started westbound on I-20. As I crossed the Chattahoochee River, I remembered that down Columbus way it forms the border between Georgia and Alabama, and in Airborne School at Fort Benning, GA we flew across it to the drop zones over in Alabama.

I found a hotel in Douglasville, ate at a Cracker Barrel, avoiding the fried okra and collard greens, and went to bed. Next morning, for the first time in my life, I had the option of choosing Instant Quaker Grits from the hotel's complimentary Continental Breakfast. I declined.

Now, mind you, I have had grits in the past, and later in the trip I was to be served okra in a salad and found it quite tasty, but I was experiencing the natural reluctance of a Yankee boy to the new and different. I had the same initial reactions to Mexican and Indian foods, both of which I now love, so don't all you Southrons get mad at me.

On the Interstate a truck almost drifted into my car, people were going at whatever speed they desired in whichever lane they chose. The whole scene was so much like Southern California that I decided to exit onto US 78, the road paralleling the highway. The Old Road.

I've used that expression a number of times, "The Old Road", and it comes from the many trips by auto we made from Providence to Vermont with my Aunt Mary, one of my mother's older sisters. She always used to point out "The Old Road" along the way until it got to be a joke with my father, an impatient man at best. (He'd point out a track in the woods and ask her if that was "The Old Road", and she'd take him seriously, and off they went.)

Anyway, in America there's always an Old Road, first an animal track, then an Indian trail, followed by a wagon road, a railroad, a highway, an Interstate, and it's always wonderful for me to contemplate the feet, the wheels that have followed those paths. I'm probably the one in a hundred who thinks of that as we all travel down the highway intent on our destinations. Well, folks, as a matter of fact, it's NOT all about Getting There. It's all about GOING There.

It seemed that I was less of an observer and a reporter and more of a philosopher as the trip ground on. That didn't stop me from wondering, though, as I passed through a small town in Georgia and saw the billboard for the local bank featuring their blonde loan officer named Candy Glaze. No philosophical thoughts there, no sireee. I thought it a name more fit for a stripper.

Back in the hinterland of the Midwest, I had noticed many houses with unused front doors. Here, in Georgia I saw a beautiful big brick Colonial home with dormer windows, shutters and a lovely front door with steps leading down to…grass. Go figure.

Other random thoughts as I drove towards Alabama:

- There was a Pancho Villa Mexican Restaurant in Bremen, GA. That surprised me.

- The Standard Enzyme Company was located in a small brick building by the railroad tracks in Bremen, across the street from the Gandy Dancers Coffee Shop. I didn't stop because I didn't need any enzymes.

- The Talley Valley campground was outside of Tallapoosa, which may have been a lalapaloosa, but they didn't have any bottled water in the Piggly Wiggly. And there are people somewhere who think that last sentence makes perfect sense.

- Somewhere in Tallapoosa there was a Possum Snout arena and I kept seeing other references to "Possum Snout", but I never found out why.

And finally, I crossed the Alabama state line where the state law is "Lights On When Raining". Outside of Oxford, AL I spotted my first sign of kudzu, and stopped at an antique mall in town. I found, though, that most of the stuff was disappointing junk or reproductions. Across the way was another store, "Fleas & Tiques" and I was tempted but declined to enter.

By now, I wanted to get to Tuscaloosa, so I got back onto the Interstate and had a good time reading road signs. When I saw the sign for the Talledega Super Speedway at Eastaboga, I decided they'd gone too far. Where DO they come up with those names? Clever, though, was the owner of the shop in Tuscaloosa, Bow Regards.

When I finally reached Tuscaloosa, I took the bypass around town and saw what I would discover to be a common sight in the South and Southwest – the most prominent skyline feature of the University of Alabama was the football stadium. Well, what else?

PART THREE
WESTWARD HO, THE GRAND MARQUIS

BOSSIER CITY

On the day that I was to leave I found Cathi and DJ intently watching the weather reports on the Birmingham TV station. Some very unsettled weather was passing through and there was a threat of tornadoes to the north of Tuscaloosa, right where they live. I was singularly impressed by the professionalism of the reporters who calmly and coolly warned viewers of the potential dangers without the hype and histrionics of Los Angeles television, where the least threat of rain becomes "Stormwatch". As luck would have it, no tornadoes developed and, although it got windy as Hell, the front passed through and I packed the car and left in a light rain.

Tuscaloosa, and Northport, AL had been very hospitable to me. I was introduced to several genuine Southern Belles and one bimbo, and enjoyed everyone's company. I had had a deadline for getting to Alabama as Cathi had planned and scheduled her annual Christmas tree trimming party for the night after my arrival. It would have been in bad form to be late, but that was the final "must do" date on my trip and I kind of looked forward to meandering, deadline-free, the rest of the way across the country.

Cathi and DJ are native Alabamans and retired schoolteachers who earned their retirement in the Los Angeles area and who had been our cruising partners, most recently on Susan's last cruise. That one had been through the Panama Canal. They retired to a home on a point of land on Lake Tuscaloosa, where DJ has a pontoon boat and Cathi a ski-doo. We managed to cruise on DJ's boat, "Whiplash" on two of the days with nice weather. During the week that I was there, we visited the Jemison – Van de Graff Mansion, an 1862 house that is being carefully restored, and were treated to Christmas Carols during its open house played by three lovely angels with violins, any one of whom I would have brought home had she been legal. We missed, though, the music of the 5th Alabama Infantry Regiment, a band of the Confederate Army with members who looked old enough to have been original players.

We also went to the Natural History Museum on the campus of the University of Alabama and saw the Hodges Meteorite, the only meteorite known to have struck a person, Ann Hodges, in 1954. Or, for that matter, in any other year. Ann survived with bruises to her thigh and a picture of her at the museum revealed that she had truly poor taste in wallpaper.

The city of Northport is across the river from, and somewhat overshadowed by, Tuscaloosa, but not on the night of Dickens Downtown. Each year the merchants of the old town area of shops, restaurants and antique stores transform the two blocks into 19th Century England, embellished with lights, music and costumed characters. I wore a Santa hat and a red flannel shirt and asked all the ladies if they'd been good girls. Only one gave the proper answer; the rest said, "Yes," to which I replied, "Too Bad". I got a lot of laughs and one poke in the arm.

We were joined for the evening by the lovely Linda and dined at the Globe Restaurant, which was festooned with posters of Shakespeare and his plays. Our waitress wore a white shift over her jeans and a mobcap and looked the proper Victorian server. Next door we met HRH, Queen Victoria in an antique store.

Everywhere we were serenaded by groups such as the afore-mentioned 5th Infantry band, the University of Alabama Tuba Band, a Scottish pipe and drum corps, choirs from every school in town and, once again, the lovely angels with violins. As the 5th Regiment played "White Christmas",

Linda and I could not resist dancing in the street and were later approached by a lady who needed ballroom dancers for a Christmas charity event. I didn't know dancers were that rare.

At the tree trimming party, I donned a tux and met guests at the front door. I sedately asked them, "Whom shall I tell Madam is calling?" and then turned and shouted into the room, "Hey, Y'all, Connie and Brian are here!" It went over well. In that part of Alabama, very few people are used to a butler introducing guests, so I was treated to some open-mouthed looks of astonishment. In Bandon, of course, we do that all the time.

One of the high points of my Tuscaloosa visit was to get re-acquainted with Frank and Reba. Susan and I had met them on our first visit to Tuscaloosa, right after Cathi and DJ had retired.

Frank, a down-home, good ol' boy, was raised on his ancestral lands up in Fayette County, watched over by a black tenant farmer, and didn't realize his name was Frank, instead of "Damyouboy" until he was old enough to go to school. "Damyouboy, don't you go near that swamp without me, there's snakes in there."

Frank says the elderly black man was a surrogate father to him and taught him a lot: like how to rob a wasp nest with your bare hand. If you wipe your hand under your sweaty armpit before you move your hand slowly toward the wasp nest, the wasps will leave the nest and you can pop it off with your hand and have instant bait for pan fish. Understand, once you had the bait you had to take the afternoon off to go fishing. He told me a lot of other tales of questionable accuracy, though Frank claims they are true.

There was wisdom in the old man, too. One year Frank's mom decided to plant an acre of cotton for extra spending money, so Frank and the old gentlemen were out in the 100+ degree Alabama heat, hoeing the cotton. The old man wiped his brow, and gave Frank this bit of knowledge, "Damyouboy, remember this, if you don't get some education, almost everything you do in life is gonna be with a damn wooden handle."

Frank was a mechanical designer who worked at an automotive supplier factory most of his life, and finished his career as a contract designer working out of his home (he's credited to be a true workaholic), but is now retired and proudly carries a business card claiming new ownership of:

Albert Burtin
Anvil Repair Service
"If your anvil is a hurtin'
Bring it to Burtin"

(Also free marital and financial advice available)

Of course, Frank says, he can't maintain a backlog, one anvil in for repair is enough at any given time. He has one on schedule now, don't bring him any more.

Frank and Reba had a home on Lake Tuscaloosa and one day Frank chose to make a lady an "off the cuff" price on what he would take for it...next day she called and said she would take him up if he and Reba could be out in under two weeks. Since 11 days after that, they have been living in a very small apartment built into a corner of a large industrial building on their property back in the country. These temporary quarters are prior to building a house nearby on land that has been in his family for generations.

Frank's a bit more of pack rat than I am, and his building (shed) is full of odd parts from old cars, tools and a gazillion et ceteras. When Reba mentioned that he should throw away an old portable TV that was no longer working, I suggested that he probably should remove the tubes before doing so. "And the power cord," he added," I always save those for future projects." Frank swears he once threw something away, and then sure enough he needed it about 6 months later and had to go buy one… He says, "never again".

I'd like to do an inventory of Frank's building, but I know that neither he, nor I, would ever finish one. It's like when I was a kid and my mom would stop my fidgeting on a rainy day by telling me to clean out my toy box and throw away old toys. Well, I'd get to playing with some things that I'd forgotten I had and the next thing you knew, it was dinnertime, all the toys went back into the box for another rainy day and Mom knew she could pull that one on me again. I guess we never really grow up, but one thing for sure, my life is far richer for having had Frank enter it.

Now it was time to leave Alabama and, while I wasn't as far south as I'd go on the trip, as Corpus Christi was still ahead of me, nevertheless I was on the next-to-last leg, Westward, Ho, The Grand Marquis.

My goal for the day was the Shreveport area, and for a while it looked as though I would be getting a very late start. The weather got better, though, and I left in just a light rain, intending to once again avoid the Interstate, this time because I didn't want to contend with the spray of trucks in addition to the rain. I opted for US 82 towards Columbus, MS.

As usual, after spending time with others, I began to reflect on my loss as soon as I was alone and I had some emotional moments. That had happened before and it continued to happen after each time I was a guest and a guest again. It was just something I had learned to expect as each visit concluded.

I never found out if there was a lot of spray from trucks on the Interstate, but I've been on enough of them to guess. Route 82 was a four-lane with median, unpopulated by traffic and allowed for a nice smooth drive into Mississippi. Once over the state line it stopped raining and I believed I had driven "out from under" the passing front.

The drive to Mathis, and the turnoff for the Natchez Trace Parkway, was relatively uneventful. In Columbus, MS there is a sign for the Tennessee Williams birthplace. "Why was he was called "Tennessee", I wondered?

Near the Oktibbeha County line I passed over the Tennessee Tombigee waterway. Now, mind you, I am no stranger to place names derived from Native American names. In New England nearly every town is named for a town in England, and every river by its Indian name, so I'm used to words like "Narragansett" and "Woonasquatucket". But in the South, they must have had some really colorful Injuns.

Upon reaching Mathis, I turned south onto the Natchez Trace Parkway. I believed that the Natchez Trace, originally an Indian path, had been used for years by boatmen who floated down the Ohio and Mississippi to New Orleans and then trekked back, their boats unable to make the trip north until steam power made it possible. When I stopped at an information site, the brochure said the same thing. Run by the US Dept. of the Interior, I was almost disappointed that they didn't charge a fee, as I would have whipped out my Golden Age pass and gone in free.

The Parkway is a narrow, two-lane road with little or no shoulder, bordered by pines and with a 50 mph speed limit. Rand McNally designates it as a scenic route on their map, but all I saw was trees. Again. By the time I saw a sign that said, "Information – Tune Radio to 1610 AM", I had passed all the sites mentioned in the broadcast.

Very quickly, I felt that driving the road was like watching the grass grow. I suppose it's OK for a short drive, especially in spring or autumn when foliage creates a show, but for the long distance it was too much of the same thing. There were a few sights along the way, though, to keep it from being a total loss. I saw a critter cross the road that I at first took to be a small deer, but it turned out to be just a big ol' hound dog. And, at one point, I passed a dozen or so wild turkeys by the side of the road.

As I went farther and farther south, there were more leaves on the trees and, with the sun eventually coming out and backlighting them, the scenery became very colorful. About 20 miles north of Jackson the road paralleled a man made lake and my horizon widened. I felt I could breathe again. Finally, I reached the Jackson area, found a bypass road and joined I-20 westbound.

I had not been behind the wheel for a week, and in that time travel had lost a bit of its charm. I didn't realize at the time that I was just a little over half way in my total mileage for the trip, but it seemed like my attitude was shifting, that the *destination*, rather than the journey, was becoming paramount. I hoped that it was a temporary feeling. One thing for sure, I was getting tired of looking at slumbering trees.

Of course, things got more exciting on the Interstate. I passed a tractor-trailer carrying two fire rescue trucks for the Pasadena Fire Department. Were they headed to California? I crossed over the Big Black River, which was neither, and entered Bovina, MS, wondering if they counted their population in people or cows. At one point, 5 or 6 police cars, some unmarked but all with lights flashing, sped by in the opposite direction. I'd never seen that many at once except on television.

I didn't stop off at Vicksburg, having done so with Susan on a previous trip. I crossed back over the Mississippi, returning, in my mind anyway, to The West. In a swampy area off the highway I saw a sign that said "Living Water" and I wondered what kinds of living things were moving beneath its surface.

There were a number of changes to travel, now that I was in Louisiana:

- There were more cultivated fields next to the road; I hadn't seen many since Oxford, AL.

- Fan palms were growing here, the first I'd seen on the whole trip.

- Another first: I began to get bug spots on the windshield.

I took a brisk walk around a rest area and discovered how truly out of shape I was. In contrast to my lack of munchies on the southbound leg, I had plenty with me now, and realized that, while Molar Express is a cute name, I needed to diet. I finally reached the Shreveport area, found a motel in Bossier (Bo-zhur) City, played in a few casinos and broke even and considered that a victory.

DENTON

Saying farewell to Bossier City was like going home empty handed after a day's fishing: you're kind of glad you went, but you'd really rather have something to show for it. I can't think of a reason why I'd return to the area.

Bossier City sits across the Red River from Shreveport and both cities tout their casinos for miles on numerous billboards along the Interstate. I found them to be small, dingy and guarded, in every case, by some very large and threatening men who scrutinized me closely to insure that I was over 21. Well, not really, I usually got them to smile when I asked if they needed my ID.

A word about casino gambling: I am not a high roller, nor am I a frequent gambler, but I do have a background in basic arithmetic and there are some aspects to video poker gambling that have been changing. It used to be that you could go into any casino and find a straight draw poker machine, with reasonable mathematical odds to win, or lose, modestly. Greed, however, motivates both the gambler and the gambling industry. The result is "bonus" machines that give out some higher jackpots in return for lower and fewer payouts for other wins. They have taken over the ranks of poker machines, and I don't like them. I don't like getting the same payout for two pair that I get for one. It's a harder hand to get and deserves to pay more, but, as I said, greed motivates, and the machines I like to play are disappearing. That being said, I got off my soapbox, tried a few of the high stakes machines, broke even nevertheless and went to bed.

I've never really regarded Louisiana as being in "The West", and even though I'd crossed the Mississippi the day before, it wasn't until I reached the Texas state line that I felt that I was back home again, sort of. I dodged the Interstate by getting off onto US 80, a pleasant, two-lane, winding road, and as I approached a large tree, a gust of wind caused the dead and dying leaves to petal down to the highway like a snow shower, in a truly autumnal effect.

Ignoring the opportunity to take a loop around Marshall, TX, I chose instead to go straight through town on what I'd call "The Strip", a main street of fast food restaurants and chain stores. One restaurant caught my eye with their sign, "Appetites Wanted – Inquire Within". My theory is that every Texas town has a Sonic and Dairy Queen, and Marshall didn't disappoint me.

Hallsville, TX didn't disappoint me, either. It had a "Merry Christmas" sign hanging on City Hall. Evidently no one in Hallsville bothered to call the ACLU.

I have struggled with this chapter, just as I struggled with writing about Illinois. All the towns I passed through looked pretty much the same in both states. It got so that I began looking for Sonics and Dairy Queens to verify my theory, and realized I'd have to add Dollar General to the mix. I passed through Gladewater, TX whose distinguishing mark seems to be the raising of sweet potatoes. Big Sandy was proud of their football team; there were signs everywhere to that effect. Somewhere on the road I passed the Character Links Golf Course and the International Alert Academy, whatever they mean by those names. Something tells me they both have church affiliations.

I have struggled with this chapter because I didn't stop and talk to anyone, didn't get to know any of the people living in this microcosm of the Heartland of America. I'm sure that, if I had, I'd have discovered people very much like me, with values that parallel mine. Sure, they probably talk a little funny, but their hearts are in the right place, and I'm sorry I missed the chance to know any of them.

I avoided Mineola via a bypass and will never know if it is anything like Mineola, LI, NY or Minneola Road in the Mojave Desert of California. I stopped for THE stop sign in Point, TX and noticed that the only new buildings were the post office and the funeral home. Necessities both, I suppose. The McDowell Cattle Ranch has been there since 1854… didn't John Wayne establish it in one of his movies? Princeton High School was an imposing edifice in Princeton, TX. I wonder if they're the Tigers?

A very nice looking woman driving a Buick Regal had a license plate, "W30-STD". I didn't notice if she was a blonde, but her husband must have made sure she knew which oil to use. When I passed a blonde driving her SUV slowly in the left lane while talking on her cell phone, I just knew I was in the outskirts of Dallas. Metro habits again.

One note about driving in Texas. Evidently on two lane highways, when a Texan is going slowly, he pulls onto the wide shoulder to allow traffic to pass. Some drivers apparently think that someone doing the speed limit should do the same thing when they want to pass. One guy tailgated me, in a passing zone with no oncoming traffic for miles, and refused to pass. I, a Yankee, refused to pull onto the shoulder while doing 65. Other states provide turnouts for that, Texas seems satisfied with shoulders.

With that, I reached Denton and called my grandson.

I spent a delightful time with Matthew. Matt had just turned 21 and had his plate pretty full with college, photography, a band and a new girlfriend. It was wonderful to spend time with a kid whose mind was so full and yet so absorbent at the same time. For years I had watched college students do little more than protest, I think, mostly against the institutions and mores I had come to accept and regard as good. I had forgotten my own rebellion while in high school and at Brown, a rebellion that was squelched firmly at West Point, but was re-kindled when I left the Army after 6 years of active service.

I have a variety of emotions when I regard kids today. Of course, they display all the characteristics enumerated in an essay I once read. It was written 2,000 years ago in Rome and complained about teenagers in a way that sounded quite contemporary.

Kids seem to display *disdain* for the people of my generation. I, on the other hand, have a sense of sorrow for them, because they don't seem to have the time I had as a teenager, the time to think about things and about themselves. Bombarded on all sides by advertising messages, by media spins, by sound bites, by TV and films that move so fast I can't follow them, today's kids seem to have a whole lot more to cope with than I did. Add to that the speed of growing up, the discussion of subjects like sex that is so open, and it's a wonder that more kids aren't giving in to overload. Columbine was bad enough, I hope it isn't duplicated or, Lord forbid, exceeded. The whole point of the teen years is to develop one's identity, and I'm not sure today's kids have the time to do that. It seems they can only imitate whatever is popular at the moment.

We, as teenagers in the 50s, rebelled against our parents' values, sought support from our friends and peers, and generally were a pain in the ass to the older generation. Sound familiar? I suppose every generation of kids goes through that phase. Most of them grow out of it while others go to work for the ACLU, become eco-terrorists, or otherwise continue to make a pain in the ass of themselves. The point is it's part of the human condition to look to spread one's wings during the hormone-dominated years, whether you were a kid growing up in Caesar's Rome, or as an American in the 50s or the 70s or today. The only differences are not in the degree of rebellion, nor in the base values rebelled against, but in the outward manifestations of the rebellion itself. It would have been every bit as rebellious for me to play Rock 'n' Roll in the house as it is for a kid today to put a safety pin through his cheek.

But we had been encouraged to question, not necessarily to tear down. We had been taught to be polite, yet firm and insistent, to wait, perhaps, until it was our turn in power to make our changes. Did that make us a more frustrated generation? I don't know, but things seemed to change in the 1960s when extremism became an instrument for change. Demonstrations and even riots were regarded as an expression of free speech, not to mention a sanctioned opportunity to cut classes.

There is something charming about the naiveté and innocence we Americans possessed before ...what? Elvis? The Beatles? Viet Nam? It's the Information Age now. Well, maybe too much information isn't such a good thing. Life was so much simpler back then, before we all became bloody know-it-alls.

What's all that got to do with my grandson? Well, he just seemed to be a lot like I was, questioning while waiting to learn more before demanding change. Maybe he wants to provide answers as well as questions. Maybe he realized that imitation is the best form of flattery. I really love the kid.

SAN ANTONIO

I left Denton on Sunday morning. Now I was on my way to visit another West Point classmate, Tony, with whom I had worked in civilian life, but hadn't seen since the Eighties. I decided to make an overnight stop between Denton and Corpus Christi, where Tony lives, in order to visit the famed San Antonio Riverwalk and, perhaps, the Alamo.

I was intent on getting through the Dallas-Fort Worth metroplex as quickly as possible, and found myself out on the plains to their north, in gently rolling terrain of wide open prairie. I saw few houses, an occasional windmill or drilling rig and a single town in the distance. It was quite different from many of the highways in the East, all hemmed in by trees. Out here I could actually look around and see things. "Maybe the West isn't all that bad," I thought, then realized that I kept changing viewpoints and wondered if I was being plagued by education or vacillation.

I passed the city limits of Flower Mound and saw picnic tables whose shelters were in the shape of Texas longhorn steer heads. Hook 'Em, Horns. Then I passed Dale Earnheart Way, an exit for the Texas Motor Speedway. Hook 'Em, Dale. Elsewhere I had seen picnic tables sheltered by what looked like oilrigs. Imaginative people, these Texans.

As the high-rise buildings of Fort Worth appeared on the horizon, a billboard proclaiming the "Family Sedan, Texas Style" showed a 4-door pickup truck. Well, what else? I crossed the Trinity River north of Fort Worth and didn't (still don't) know if it's a famous river or not. More billboards featured Chick Fil-A ads, one with cows saying, "Feed yer herd, save ourz".

My passage through Fort Worth was uneventful.

I was headed toward Waco now, and the name used to evoke the image of a cow town, and scenes of the old west; nowadays it brings words like "infamy" and "bureaucratic stupidity" to mind. Somewhere I read that it took the U.S. forces less time to take Baghdad than it took Janet Reno to take the Branch Davidian complex. It seems to me that the politicians involved had more concern with how their actions would be perceived than with what was right and what was wrong. Harry Truman wouldn't have waited that long.

By now I was passing through wonderful countryside, occasional trees, ranches, hay fields, a new view from the top of every hill. "Hooray for Texas," I thought. This stretch, at least, was taking the monotony out of travel, and I was beginning to regain the perspective that probably makes me a Westerner. I need room. I need room to breathe, room to stretch, room to travel, and the confines of the East, in its cities and tree-lined highways just didn't give me room. All my nostalgic feelings for the East seemed swept away when I returned to the vistas of the West.

There was a gas station with gas for $1.54, the lowest price by far that I had seen anywhere, and believe it or not, I turned around and back-tracked to fill up. In the old days, i.e., before retirement, I would have kept going in the belief that another station down the road would price it even lower, but this time, I turned around. (As it turned out, this was the lowest price I saw for gas anywhere on my 12,043-mile trip.) The gas station was situated along with the Czech Bakery in West, TX. The gas was cheap, the pastry expensive, who'd a thunk it?

Well, come on, they MIGHT have tried to lure you in to buy expensive gas with a sign, "Cheap Pastry", eh?

One thing I noticed around the country, and here in Texas, too, was that every Cracker Barrel restaurant I passed had a full parking lot. Buy their stock.

I passed up the chance to visit the Texas Ranger Museum in Waco, but did note that the city seems to have a nicely developed riverfront. There were lots of spires on the east side of the Interstate, but I couldn't tell if they were churches or university buildings.

As I continued on, I once again commented into the tape recorder that "gently rolling terrain" was a tiresome phrase, but I didn't know how else to describe the pleasant land I was driving through. The word "undulating" makes me think of a belly dancer.

I spotted a couple of old style longhorns feeding on hay in front of a Westinghouse plant and wondered if they were corporate pets.

At about this point, I realized that there had been a gradual change in my comments from the first seven tapes of my journey; that I had gone from plain reporting to something else. Instead of doing a travelogue, I was now editorializing, or, if you will, philosophizing. I'd had a lot of time to reflect upon people whom I hadn't seen for many years; and, while I'd tried to avoid thinking about it, upon my own situation of widowhood.

On the one hand, I'd always thought that I would have to be a demonstrable success to my friends; that I would have to live up to the potential that I, and a lot of others, had foreseen. I had believed that I would be accepted only if I had lived up to their expectations.

Instead, I found that most others had struggled through life as I had, along different paths, of course, but struggled nevertheless. In my case I had gone through life with little or no self-esteem, the product of a domineering father. West Point and Army service were supposed to fix me, but didn't. Lots of other things were supposed to fix me, also, but didn't. I had to find out that only I could fix me, with the repetition of the Serenity Prayer. Many repetitions, and I'm still saying it.

As I mentioned earlier the trappings of position and prestige meant little to any of us now. Maybe that's the definition of true friendship. I could hear the sound of my sacred cows falling over, and yea, verily, it was loud unto my ears.

On the other hand, I was beginning to come to grips with my grief. It was real, it was palpable and it reared its head each time I stopped being a guest again and moved on. I felt like the character in the Li'l Abner comic strip who had the perpetual cloud over him. Though I sometimes walked in sunshine, I was never able to escape the darkness.

Anyway, I passed Buda, TX and wondered if there's a Pest.

I reached San Antonio after a lot of driving into the sun. I rejoiced in my decision to not try for Corpus in one day, found my hotel and went out to explore. The hotel, in an old jail building recently renovated, was about six or seven blocks from the Alamo, and less from the famed Riverwalk. I was struck by two things about the downtown area I walked through – first, it has the capacity to become grubby overnight yet is very clean, at least in the sense that it's free of trash and debris. But there is OLD dirt there; dirt worn into the pavements and the sidewalks and it's easy to see that, without constant care, San Antone could get really dingy very quickly.

Second, most of the businesses I passed were His-panic in name, either as mercantile or restaurant establish-ments. Most of the pedestrians were Hispanic as well, and those who weren't were obviously tourists, but I didn't hear a great deal of Spanish being spoken. Face it; many of these people have probably been in this country longer than the Siedzicks, by far.

As I mentioned, I am a second-generation American, a product of two families that immigrated in the early 1900s. In those days, immigrants wanted nothing more than to assimilate. My grandparents sent my mother and father and their siblings to school to learn English and to become full citizens of the country in which they'd been born. My parents refused to teach me Polish and insisted that we were all Americans, immersed in American culture. Polish traditions were celebrated on some holidays, mostly at Christmas and Easter, but as Americans, we celebrated Thanksgiving and the Fourth and partied equally heartily.

Was it a good thing that I was deprived of a Polish heritage? I sometimes wonder, when I hear about the richness of other families that retain some of their old ways. On the other hand, I am nearly sickened when I see Americans bending over for foreigners in our country, many of whom are here illegally, refuse to learn our language and have to have things spelled out for them in their own. I strongly resent being told by the telephone to "Press 1 to continue in English." Why not press something to hear it in some other language, why do I have to perform an action just to hear my native tongue? I've resolved to boycott any company that uses that type of message.

I have heard comments about the Alamo that it was very small. Well, that is certainly true of the mission church, used in all the photographs as the icon of the Alamo, but the grounds and walls are actually quite extensive. At least they seemed extensive to me when trying to imagine defending the walls with only a few hundred men with muzzle-loading, single-shot flintlocks. I bought my requisite book at the museum gift shop where they had a lot of actual mementos of Crocket and Bowie. I didn't see anything belonging to

Travis, but then, I didn't see everything. My buddy, Bob, would have.

San Antonio's Riverwalk is impressive, charming and enchanting. I actually ran out of adjectives (adverbs?) in trying to describe my feelings about it. I was utterly taken with the place. I had not envisioned it as being two stories below street level, but it is. Planted in lush vegetation, it was quite cool to walk along, compared to the street where it must have been 80 degrees. And remember, it seldom goes above 70 in Bandon. I decided to spend the rest of the afternoon in a cool nap in my room and leave more exploration of the Riverwalk for when I went out to dinner.

Oh, the Riverwalk at night is marvelous! It filled my senses with sights and sounds and smells. 'Twas the season and the boats were filled with children singing Christmas carols; the young Girl Scouts who sat across the aisle from me at the Café Ole' said they were in a troop that sang every year and then came to dinner. Their moms were two tables down, enjoying their own tradition.

The architecture along the Riverwalk is rich and varied: from old stone to brick to Spanish stucco with wrought iron railings and balconies. Every staircase leading to street level is architecturally different as is every bridge crossing over the river. Plantings include monstrous trees at river level growing 4 or 5 stories high, festooned for the holidays with colored lights; various shrubs along the walk add to the greenery. Fountains here and there and miniature waterfalls add to the coolness and ambience. After writing this paragraph I began to wonder if I should enter the travel magazine business.

I don't know when I've been in a more romantic spot than the Riverwalk at night. Sections of it are bright and noisy, other sections are quiet and dark enough for romance but not for nefarious skullduggery. Jaded Peter was impressed.

I was in no rush to leave on Monday morning, as my friend Tony teaches school in Corpus Christi and wouldn't be available until 2 PM, so I took another stroll, this time with camera in hand, to the Alamo and the Riverwalk and later discovered I had shot 66 pictures. Oh, the wonder of digital photography!

It was a bright, clear day, but the temperature had dropped from the previous day's 80 to about 51. The natives were huddled in parkas, gloves and scarves whilst I, child of New England and the Northwest, was comfortable in a shirt and windbreaker. The early morning sun made for great angles and illumination everywhere I went, and I behaved like a kid in a candy shop with my camera. I got back to the hotel just in time for checkout.

I chose to leave San Antonio right down one of its main streets, Flores, which turned into US 281 heading south towards Corpus Christi. 281 went to Pleasanton and then to I-37. The south side of San Antonio was rather run down, but with clean streets and a lot of appliance stores, most with appliances sitting out in the cold. I guess it doesn't rain very much in San Antone.

The main drag of Pleasanton had a Dairy Queen, but no Sonic and no Dollar General, so I will not hereafter refer to it as a typical Texas town. After all, Bandon has a Dairy Queen. Pleasanton did, however, have lamppost decorations of angels with trumpets alternating with bells, clearly religious symbols heralding the coming of the Winter Equinox, and I wondered how they could get away with it, and rejoiced that they did.

OK, let's get it out in the open. Last time I looked, over 80% of the people in the United States professed to believe in God; yet the less than 20% who do not have buffaloed us into believing that we have violated their rights if we allow school prayer, or any symbol of our belief in a public place.

They harp on the "separation of church and state" provisions of the Constitution. But anyone who has read American History realizes that the separation was from a state-sponsored church, not from a belief in God. What the HELL ever happened to majority rule? I once received the suggestion that I, and everyone I knew, should send a Christmas card to the ACLU. I got the idea too late for that Christmas, but resolved to do it in coming years until those people come to their senses.

Anyway, a sign for food led me off US 281 onto Alt US 281 through Carrolton, TX (pop 179) and Stetson's Café. The café turned out to be four tables in a small store selling candy and a few canned goods. No menus, but a board listing the available sandwiches. I had a chicken breast, served on white toast with lettuce, tomato and onion and coffee that…well, let's not talk about the coffee. The sandwich was OK. After the owner/waitress/cook/cashier spotted me for a stranger and asked which way I was going, she directed me back to the freeway. As if I could have gotten lost. There's one road into town and one road out. Paved, that is. I passed a mission style church and went through rolling ranch land and open prairie, saw a water hole with a white crust of salt around it, and entered Live Oak County. By now you may know how I feel about Live Oaks.

After re-joining I-37, I spotted the exit for Swinney Switch. Some day I'm gonna take it. There was a beautiful Spanish two-story hacienda named Windward Ranch that was absolutely gorgeous. About 20 miles out of Corpus Christi, the land flattened and, as Susan would have said, "There were flat fertile fields lying fallow." I wouldn't have said that, as I always avoid annoying alliteration.

I finally spotted some fields that weren't fallow; they held cotton. I followed Tony's directions to his home and pulled into his driveway one minute before my scheduled arrival time of 2 PM. What a guy.

AMARILLO

Corpus Christi is a tremendously busy place, but I just can't imagine what all those people do for a living; there are plenty of retail establishments, a relatively small downtown business area, and no visible manufacturing. The people I saw were predominantly Hispanic, spoke rapid-fire English that sounded like rapid-fire Spanish, and were difficult for me to understand, and the abundance of palm trees and the otherwise flat, open area reminded me of Los Angeles. I don't want to live there.

My friend, Tony, was my next-door neighbor while at the 82d Airborne Division. Once, while barbequing for both families on a Sunday, he laughed when I received a call that I had to go to XVIII Airborne Corps Headquarters to pick up a classified message for our Division. I worked at Division Headquarters at the time and got the last laugh when the message turned out to be a requirement to send troops to the Congo and, though I had nothing to do with it, Tony was assigned to lead them.

Tony and I both received orders to Panama in 1965; I went to an Airborne battalion and he to the School of The Americas. Conditions were a lot more primitive at the posts on the Atlantic side, where he was assigned, so Tony opted for an unaccompanied tour and only saw Gayle when she came down on a tourist visa. My wife and daughters did come down for my three-year tour and my son was born there.

Tony had not changed a bit, extending his boyish exuberance and optimism about EVERYTHING into his 60s. He took me on tours of the area, played golf with me and even hosted me aboard a gambling ship that went out beyond the limit, rolled in the wind-swept shallow waters and gave me a case of seasickness. As I was lying on a banquette, a drunk fell and sat on my head. Besides that, I lost money.

Tony rescued me from the drunk and later proposed that he and I buy a beachside condo, for my full-time use in winter and his family's occasional use the rest of the year. I declined, but continue to think about it. Through my entire visit, Tony's wonderful wife Gayle continued to exhibit the same forbearance she has for shown for years.

When I left Corpus Christi, I was backtracking for the second time on the journey, along I-37 on my way back to San Antonio, with Denver as my ultimate destination. I had thought to try for Abilene, TX, but the distance was a bit far for my late start. I had played a last round of golf with Tony and his buddies and was now tired; with an early afternoon departure, Junction, TX, on I-10 looked like it would be my first day's end.

I didn't record much on the road back to San Antone except to note that there was a lot of prairie and little cropland there, scrub brush and prickly pear cactus made a lot of stuff for cattle to get lost in. Small gullies abounded and I guessed that these were the famed "breaks" that Louis L'Amour wrote about in his novels, places where it was difficult to find and remove cattle. And I noted Peggy, TX and wished I'd stopped for a postcard to send to my sister.

After circling San Antonio and picking up I-10 I noticed a ridgeline and wondered if it was the cap rock or rim rock or whatever they call it in Texas where the state suddenly drops from one level to another. I never found a map to tell me so, but once I ascended the line of cliffs, I found the country to be quite hilly and assumed I was in Texas' Hill Country. Soon a small dry streambed called the Hill Country Raceway confirmed it.

There were exits for Welfare, TX and Comfort, TX and I wondered what was involved in moving from one to the other. In this region there seemed to be a lot of similarities to areas in California; I saw the same brown grass and the same occasional trees looking like California oaks. There were runs here and there where water flowed at one time or another during the year; the whole effect gave me a familiar feeling, even though I'd never been to this part of Texas before.

There may be a lot of junctions in Texas, but there's only one Junction. It has a Dairy Queen and I never got far enough into town to find out if there were a Sonic or Dollar General. Anyway, Junction, "The Front Porch of The West". "Reunion Capital of Texas". Located at the junction of I-10 and US 83, which led south to Uvalde.

Where in the world had I ever heard of Uvalde? Friend Bob later informed me that Uvalde was the site of the last train robbery in the U.S. True or not, it's on the road to Del Rio, Don Imus' famed "Gold Buckle of the Bible Belt." I have never been to either town; don't expect that I ever will.

When I stopped at the local gas station to fill up, I noticed that there was "Deer Corn" for sale outside in 40 lb bags. I asked about that and the young clerk said that hunters spread the feed all year long to lure the deer to a particular spot so that they can shoot them once the season opened. I didn't think that was very sporting, and said so, especially since we kill more deer on the highways each year than by hunting. "Yes," she said, "I got an 8 point buck with my car."

I could not get a local number for access to the Internet, so I was left with other means of amusing myself in my motel room until my early morning departure for Amarillo. Like watching some truly dreadful TV programs, an activity that had become a fact of life on the road. As a result, I got to sleep early and got an early start out of Junction.

I drove north on US 83 towards Eden, and noted that, in general, Texas gives good road; 83 was wide shouldered to allow for passing, provided that the passee knows the local customs and pulls over. Farther south, I had been plagued by drivers who pulled into the passing lane, only to take forever to pass. It still amazes me that some drivers will actually

SLOW DOWN when passing a truck. Get past him and out of danger, I says.

The sun came up as I was driving north and lit the tops of the trees, a brief illumination of my passage. I drove through Menard, site of some stone buildings, lots of goats in pastures, and entered Concho County, a Boll Weevil Free Area, with an enforced quarantine and a $500 fine if caught trafficking in boll weevils. Not me, sir.

The country flattened and opened up as I switched to US 87 towards San Angelo and eventually I was in desert. A map at a rest area told me I had transited from the Hill Country to The Panhandle Plains, and that meant that I had visited, at one time or another in my life, every section of Texas except the Big Bend Plains.

After crossing Kickapoo Creek, which had a lot of water in it, though from where I couldn't tell, I reached cotton country. US 87 became a four-lane road with a grassy median, as wide as an Interstate and without trucks.

I entered Tom Green County, whoever he was, passed an entrance to Goodfellow AFB, a training center for intelligence, fire fighting and instruments for the Air Force and entered the grubby outskirts of San Angelo. The center of town was pretty clean and looked relatively new, though, and there was an attractive Visitor Center on the banks of the Rio Concho.

Why, I wondered, were all the names of the rivers in Texas so familiar to me? Must have been from all the westerns I watched as a kid, hearing names that some Hollywood screenwriter pulled off a map of Texas. Or maybe it was the influence of Louis L'Amour again.

Outside of San Angelo, I slowed down to a 60 speed limit to pass through Carlsbad, TX, site of the San Angelo State School. It didn't look too confining, but it reminded me of Socanosset, the state school for boys in Rhode Island. When I was growing up, parents kept their kids in line by asking, "You wanna go to Socanosset?" You never wanted to confront a kid who'd been there; they chewed nails, and you knew you'd be doomed.

I passed up the chance to go into the Montvale cemetery, noted by a historical marker, and couldn't find an Internet reference to it later. I still don't know who's buried there. Sterling City's FFA welcomed me to a predominantly brick town and then I hit oil country as I approached Big Spring; working oil pumps were everywhere, about a hundred yards apart, and wind turbines were there as well. I saw a large building in the distance and guessed it to be a VA hospital. It was! And, lo, it had a big sign, "Peace on Earth" on top. Isn't that a religious message?

As I began to fight a crosswind and dodge tumbleweeds, yet another Texas driver pulled out to pass a truck in front of me and seemed to forget why he was there. Maybe he lost his nerve. Sure didn't give me the confidence in Tall Texans I got from watching Hopalong Cassidy movies. I raced a dust storm coming from my left and found myself driving through cotton fields with curved rows, planted, I assumed, to avoid wind erosion. In their midst, an oil drill rig was working and I actually saw some roughnecks. One kid looked like a young John Wayne.

Soon enough, I was in Lubbock and, not soon enough, I was on the other side. It's true. Happiness IS Lubbock in the rear view mirror.

Some other noticeables of note:

- A store titled Antiques and Cherishables.

- A truck carrying baked goods, Mrs. Bairds, Texas Born, Texas Bread.

- Lubbock, pop 201,000. I wonder why?

- Levelland, TX and Floydada, TX. I wonder why?

- Lubbock International Airport. International, mind you.

- A rest area on I-27 with a sign, "Comfort Station". I hadn't seen that term in print since I was a kid in Providence, RI.

Once north of Plainview, TX, an aptly named place if ever I saw one, I was officially in The Panhandle; to the east of me was Oklahoma. I passed the exit for Happy, TX, wondering what could make me happy, sitting out in the middle of this flat-assed prairie.

Canyon, TX has signs for the Palo Duro state park, once, I believe, the stronghold of the Comanches, and now also home of the Panhandle Plains Museum. I skipped both.

Amarillo ain't Lubbock.

DENVER, AGAIN

The sky was dark and overcast on a frosty morning as I left Amarillo, snow showers were in the forecast and I hoped to avoid them as I crossed the Texas and Oklahoma Panhandles and entered southeastern Colorado. I missed my turnoff for US 87/287 and had to backtrack on the freeway.

One aspect of Texas Interstates, or freeways, that I haven't noticed elsewhere in the nation, is the special U-turn lanes at exit ramps that allow a driver to move from the service road in one direction to the service road in the other without having to contend with traffic lights. "Good for Texas," I thought, as I got headed in the right direction.

I had stayed in the nicest and least expensive room of my trip in Amarillo, a town that seems under-populated for its road system. Well, Lubbock is, too, I guess, but...

Quickly, I was out on the Panhandle Plains, with long wide valleys and gentle slopes, where I could literally see for leagues. I also now began to feel dryness in my lips as the aridity of the West began to affect them. I'd certainly noticed that in Denver on my previous visit, along with some dryness in my eyes.

I finally reached the point where I had to use a tape that I had already recorded on this trip, because I'd gone through all ten that I'd brought with me. Of course, I'd transcribed this one and saved it in the laptop, so it was good for re-use. It seemed like I'd recorded a lot, but much of what I'd taped was drivel, sometimes I just picked up the recorder and spoke for the sake of talking because I was lonely. Susan had been a wonderful traveling companion, and I missed the light-hearted banter, and the wonder in her voice when she saw new places.

She was a lover of her language and took pride in speaking the Queen's English. I have already alluded to her love of alliteration, and we sometimes made a game of it on the road. She also had a calendar that I had given her, filled with obscure or archaic words and tried to work them into common use. Susan teased me about writing a novel, "Mools (grave earth) Of The Clamjaffry (rabble, mob)". She was sure it would sell on the title alone. Well, I know I'd have to pick it up just to find our what it meant. God, how I missed her!

I crossed the Canadian River, an old friend from many trips on I-25 in New Mexico, and wondered if it flowed from here to there, or from there to here. At this point, the highway was a great one, as good as an Interstate, and the only truck I'd seen on it pulled off. Mapquest, which has a love affair with Interstates, had suggested I-40 to I-25 as the way to get from Amarillo to Denver. Perhaps that's true for truckers, but I decided that route stunk, and one glance at a map will tell you it sure isn't a straight line.

A large plant loomed in the distance and when I drew abreast I noted that the road was signed "Helium Plant Road". I drew the obvious conclusion and then passed a very large natural gas transfer plant. The low underbrush of the prairie gave way to yucca and cholla and "prairie" no longer described what I call a desert. I have no idea why those facilities chose the Panhandle, but they obviously were the only means of employment for the folks who live out there.

At Dumas, pop. 13,000, the highways diverged, 87 going off west into New Mexico and 287 continuing towards Colorado. Dumas had a fine main street ideal for cruising, was big enough for a Wal-Mart, and had at least one country girl who knows how to drive like a city girl – she got the jump on me at a changing traffic light and made an oncoming left turn in front of me. Dumas has a branch of the

Happy State Bank and its Sonic and Dairy Queen are opposite one another on Main Street. Other than that...

Outside of town, I passed a big John Deere place and finally hit an agricultural belt, saw a concern specializing in sorghum and other grains (what is it that we use sorghum for?), lots of grain storage and numerous oil wells pumping. There were natural gas stations as well, and I detected the odor of gas in the air, reminding me of Eastern New Mexico.

At Cactus, TX, there were large grain silos everywhere, rail cars everywhere, and singlewide trailer homes everywhere. A working plant had the sign "Swift & Co., Cactus Beef Plant" and I figured I had found the major source of employment in town.

By now my instincts were telling me that I was gaining elevation ever so slowly and gently, while my intellect was saying, "Of course, Dummy, you're going up to about 4,000 feet elevation by the time you reach Colorado." But since I was in the flattest country I'd been in on my entire trip, the changes were imperceptible. Could Kansas be worse?

At a watering tank, cattle were standing in the water up to their knees, they just couldn't stay outside and drink, they had to get in and play just like little kids. I stopped in Stratford, TX, home of the Stratford Elks, to make a phone call and couldn't get a cell signal. I wanted to let Mary Ellen know that I was leaving Texas. At last.

It was all virgin road and I was glad I'd done it. Once. I'd always wanted to see the Texas Panhandle, and now that I had, I'd no desire to see it again. As I approached the Oklahoma state line, the clouds began to break up in the distance and blue sky appeared in patches, and I began to think of other things, like lunch.

The highway narrowed to two lanes as I entered Oklahoma and drove through, guess what, gently rolling terrain. There was a traffic circle to navigate in Boise City,

OK, and a sign for Denver, 288 miles. North of town there were farms, ranches and natural gas stations, no oil pumps.

Cattle were feeding in many of the crop fields, separated from the roadway by a single strand of low-strung electric fence. Out in the middle of nowhere I spotted an historical marker for the Santa Fe Trail. I crossed the Cimarron River, another river I had seen in New Mexico, here it was holding very little water, but had a large flood plain.

Shortly after my Welcome to Colorful Colorado, I entered Campo, CO, elev. 4,339 feet and my instincts and intellect both proved to be right, I had gained altitude. Lots of it.

Despite living for almost 13 years in Denver, I had never gone to the southeastern corner of Colorado. I'd poked my nose into many another corner, but not this one. There were a lot of cattle grazing in fields with grass up to their bellies and I wasn't surprised to find that Springfield, CO was home of the Longhorns. Springfield, if you didn't know it, is the most popular name for a town among our 48 states. I don't know if there is a Springfield, Alaska or Springfield, Hawaii, but I doubt it.

North of Springfield there was a large conical hill to my right front that slowly evolved into a double hill with a saddle. No signs indicated what it might be called, but the map showed a place name in the vicinity as "Two Buttes". Made sense to me. Even further north was a line of wind turbines, the largest I'd seen since California. I commented into the tape recorder as I drew abreast of Two Buttes that they weren't flat buttes at all, but were pointed, and shaped like a young woman's breasts, even that one was larger than the other. I said I doubted that I would put that in print. So I did.

I pulled off at a rest stop and spotted some unique rock formations, took out the camera and made the last scenic pictures of my trip. I was impressed with the clear, clean smell of the air here in Colorado, as always. I was not impressed with the pavements, though; the roads seemed the worst I'd encountered in a long while.

At Lamar, I listened to Prudence Dictates and topped off the tank of the car as the sky was getting darker and I didn't want to have to gas up in whatever might be falling soon.

Lamar was a valuable source of wonderful information:

- The Best Western in Lamar is named the Cow Palace.

- Lamar is on the Santa Fe Trail, which must mean that in Colorado, the trail goes due north-south, since I had seen a few other markers before, to the south.

- A time/temperature clock reminded me that I had entered the Mountain Time Zone.

- The Arkansas River was barely a trickle in Lamar; the map showed a lake further upstream, the river must be dammed.

Lamar's elevation is only 3,600 feet, so I had dropped down a bit to enter the Arkansas Valley. I got back to altitude at Eads, elev. 4,213, but only seemed to encounter rail cars with rusting wheels and rusting farm equipment outside of town. I was in prairie, now, wide open with only a few trees in the watercourses.

Eads hosts the Kiowa County Fair. Shortly after, I was in Cheyenne County and later, I knew, I'd enter Arapahoe County. The early settlers of Colorado didn't like their Injuns, but they seem to have named a lot of counties for them. Go figure.

After passing a place called Wild Horse, about a dozen dwellings and a post office, I found I could see Pike's Peak in the distance. I reached I-70 near Limon and stopped for a rest and some lip balm, then continued on I-70 a short distance to CO 86, which would bring me into the south side of the Denver metro area, where I planned to stay the night.

In Elbert County I began to see snow on the ground, the first I'd seen since leaving New Hampshire. I gained altitude as I drove west to Kiowa, and pine trees appeared before I reached town, elev. 6,347. Elizabeth, a little higher, had been a fashionable place to live for city "escapees" back in the 80s, but didn't look so great to me now.

I crossed Running Creek, which was, reached Frank-town and took CO 83 north to Parker and on into Aurora, paralleling Cherry Creek. The area was barely recognizable after the buildup of 30 years. The sleepy towns are now full grown bedroom communities for Denver and the formerly two lane state highway is, in some places, as large as 6 lanes.

Building was going on in the flood plain of Cherry Creek and there is not, as far as I know, any flood control on the creek. A dam washed out in the 30s during a flash flood and I don't think anything was built to replace it. If ever there is a tragedy, the homeowners will undoubtedly wail, like the Californian hill dwellers, "Nobody told us…" Well, folks, there's a reason it's called a flood plain, and I remember TV stories of mudslides in California in the 50s.

I passed the Emerald Isle, a trendy restaurant that sits on the site of a shot-and-beer place that Tony and I considered buying in the 70s. Of course, the place is, and has been, a gold mine, but not for us. I reached my motel and breathed a sigh of relief that I had made the trip from the Gulf Coast to the Rockies without incident.

TUCSON

Denver greeted me with an inch of snow overnight and single digit temperatures. I harked back to the radiator flush I got at the family-run place in Rochester, IN and was grateful.

I had recorded my trip through the Panhandle with the notice of two things, sky and flat, and I looked forward to seeing the Rocky Mountains. It would be days before they put in an appearance, but the good thing about Denver weather is its changeability. Soon enough, there was sunshine, the snow melted, the mountains showed up and I proceeded to enjoy Christmas with friends and family.

My son, Mike, was discharged from the Army at last. Though he would continue in the Reserve, he now had the opportunity to enjoy his "terminal leave" before reporting back to his regular job. I stayed with Mike and Laura and their two boys through Christmas day and was overjoyed to watch Sean and Cameron, ages 5 and 3, open their Christmas presents with all the wonder and delight that I expected. Mike and I got to spend a good bit of time together and, much to my own delight, I discovered that I'd gotten smart. I guess 64 *is* the magic age.

On my last day with Mike, he warned me that he was catching a head cold and, sure enough, I came down with one, too. It was to curtail my activities for over a week, as I tried to fight it off with Nyquil, Dayquil, immune system boosters and incantations taught me by a crone I once dated in Southern California.

In spite of the head cold, I went back up to Fort Collins for a second look at a property I'd liked, but it didn't have the same appeal, the numbers weren't making sense, and the large-breasted realtor was off duty. I left Fort

Collins timing myself to be behind the Denver rush hour traffic and set off down I-25 for New Mexico.

A large Pacific storm was plaguing Southern California and moving east and it looked like I might encounter bad weather along the way if it moved faster than I could. Ominous dark clouds framed the Rockies, but the Front Range and the highway remained in sunshine throughout the drive. I passed through Denver in 22 minutes and made note that people who complain about Denver traffic should serve a little time in L.A.

I was following a very familiar route. Years before, when Mike was a cadet at the New Mexico Military Institute in Roswell, I had combined pleasure with business and taken trips down from Denver to see him before going over to Albuquerque on sales calls. Almost nothing had changed, except for the speed limit, now up to 75 in both Colorado and New Mexico. I used to make the trip when it was 55, watchful of the Colorado troopers who converged on the last 50 miles of Interstate between Walsenburg and Raton Pass.

I got through Colorado Springs, which I had always hated for its traffic, and which didn't disappoint me this time. I re-crossed the Arkansas River at Pueblo, and saw the furnaces of CF&I Steel standing as silent reminders of a past that once illuminated America's greatness. Is anyone making steel in the United States anymore?

Dark clouds over the mountains persisted and warned me away from the La Veta Pass-Fort Garland-Santa Fe route that is prettier than I-25, but more likely to be treacherous in snow. Raton Pass was still there, still high and still a pass, still separating Colorado from New Mexico. I crossed the Canadian River again, saw Wagon Mound, a familiar sight from many previous trips, and decided to bed down in Las Vegas, NM. I had stopped twice for short naps and measures of Dayquil, but I was pooped and I gave up hope that I could reach Albuquerque, my intended destination.

Las Vegas, NM bears no resemblance to its Nevada namesake, unless one might want to view Sin City as it might have been in the 40s, pre-Bugsy. I collapsed for a few hours in a hotel room, and then went out in search of dinner and a new bottle of Nyquil, since mine had opened in my suitcase and ruined a pair of slippers and soaked a sweatshirt. Vegas by night didn't look too bad. A lot of folks still had their Christmas lights burning and the streets looked clean. I don't know if I'd be as impressed in daylight.

"Las Vegas" in Spanish means "the meadows" and the city in Nevada was so named because springs in the area had watered a few acres of grass. I have no idea why the name applied to the New Mexican city, but I suspect there are some meadows lurking somewhere in town.

Next day, I encountered some strong winds as I aimed for Las Cruces, NM, once again needing naps and cold remedies. I recorded very little about this leg of the trip: getting there was paramount and recording a journey with my senses dulled wasn't even secondary.

Nevertheless, I noted that Santa Fe, at 7,000 or more feet, was probably the highest I would be on the rest of the journey. I congratulated myself on being "West of The Pecos" (there was a book, "West of the Pecos" or a repeated phrase in a movie, and I used to tell my son we were west of the Pecos whenever we crossed the river in New Mexico, or Pecos Street in Denver). Junipers festooned with silvery garlands were in the median strip north of Albuquerque, a strange desert celebration of Christmas.

I breezed through town and was surprised when I crossed the Rio Grande. I knew Las Cruces was on the east side of the river and hadn't expected to cross it until then. But later, I re-crossed, entered the agricultural section of the Rio Grande valley and saw lots of green fields and pecan orchards. I reached Las Cruces, collapsed again, and rested for the final leg to Tucson.

I gathered literature on Las Cruces as a potential winter retreat, thinking now that I could stay with Bandon as a summertime place, and perhaps locate somewhere else in the winters. As I left town, I spotted a hot air balloon off to my right, slowly ascending in the quiet morning air. I crossed, once again, the Rio Grande, which was now barely a trickle, thanks to all the agricultural usage, and made my way west into the desert.

I-10 just seems to be one of those roads that can annoy me wherever I encounter it. Here, west of Las Cruces, it was similar to stretches in Southern California: it was made of concrete slabs that had shifted ever so slightly to cause the snick-snick of the tires that I find really bothersome. Patched patches didn't help. About the time I finished bitching about the road surface into my tape recorder, the road turned to asphalt and the problem went away. Am I a problem solver, or what?

There were a few Border Patrol agents chatting with a civilian at the Border Control Point. Their body language signaled an air of familiarity about the conversation. I wondered if he was an informant or a "coyote" who was traveling empty-handed.

Out in the desert west of Deming, I saw a train full of ocean-going containers and it once again brought home to me what a marvelous bunch the pioneers were who first crossed this desert on foot. Nowadays we whiz everything a family could have needed for life on one flatcar across the desert at 60 miles an hour. In those days, they trudged along at the speed of the slowest member in their party.

The Continental Divide is at 4,585 feet; in a region so flat there was no way one could tell it was really dividing anything. Just the same, I was now on the western slope of the United States, where I had not been since Wyoming, several months earlier.

There were a lot of snowbirds heading west, mounted high in their RVs, possibly heading to Yuma, a wintertime Mecca, and I didn't envy their gas bills as they fought a strong westerly wind. I didn't envy mine, either, but there's still a lot of square, boxy wind-resistant RVs out there, and I just don't know how they manage to get anywhere.

I passed up the side road to Tombstone, where I've been, noted that I-10 is the Pearl Harbor Memorial Highway and coasted into Tucson for a visit with Rex and Sandy.

PASADENA

I stayed in Tucson for nearly a week, disappointing my hosts, I'm sure, because I arrived with a cold and left barely cured.   Fortunately, I must have been past the contagious stage because neither Rex nor Sandy caught anything.

Rex and Sandy had retired to Tucson from Denver, where I had known them from the 70s. I have known three guys named Rex in my life, one at West Point and the other two working for the same company with me in Denver.

The Southwest continued to be plagued by Pacific storms, and it curtailed a lot of the activities I would have enjoyed. A visit to Davis-Monthan AFB was out of the question because it was an all-day affair, and we never had a full day without rain. We did get to hike in one of the area's desert parks, and visited a local Indian casino where I earned enough gas money to go to Laughlin. Other than that, I mostly hung out and met neighbors.

Rain in Southern California had turned the area into a miserable place and my plan to visit the other Rex, and Marie in Ramona, CA, had to be canceled because he had also caught a respiratory something. Besides, their golf course was unplayable. We decided to postpone that visit, and I changed course for Laughlin, NV.

With the visit to Rex and Marie cancelled, I put an end to my freeloading there in Tucson. It was just as well; I was beginning to long for home. The trip had been wonderful and seeing old friends and family had been heartwarming. I still had some family to see in Pasadena, but I wouldn't be staying with any of them. I would not be a guest again.

By now I had realized that leaving Bandon had not cured any ache in my heart for the loss of Susan, travel had merely postponed the moments when I would be alone to grieve. Those had mostly come when I was in the car, after having been a guest. It got no easier; despite the distractions of company, the hollowness remained and it didn't seem to lessen with miles or time.

When I was in the 82d Airborne Division, I worked with a sergeant whose favorite saying in tough circumstances was, "Take up the slack and drive on." And that's all there was left for me to do. Take up the slack and drive on. Not a bad motto for life.

I headed out of Tucson on I-10 West, actually traveling north towards Phoenix. Somewhere out to the west I could see a lot of large airplanes parked, about 40 or so of them and I wondered why. They looked to be civilian airliners, and I had no idea why they were there.

Further on, Picacho Peak, a ragged stone upthrust in the Arizona desert, looked as though it had to have been worshipped as a phallus at some point in history. Maybe it still is. Rex and Sandy had told me that the saguaro cactus was native only to the Tucson area, in the northern edge of the Sonoran Desert, and that all other saguaros had been planted. I had seen them coating the desert north of Phoenix and now, as I looked at fields of saguaro on Picacho Peak, I found their claim a little hard to believe.

The desert still held no great promise for me. There was a time when I used to wonder if this canyon held a lost gold mine, or if there might be hidden water in those mountains, but my days of wanting to emulate the one-burro prospector and investigate all those forbidding niches are over. I no longer envy anyone who does.

After spotting rows of pecan trees 50 miles north of Tucson and wondering where their water came from, I decided to count up the states I'd traveled through on this trip, since Arizona was the last new one I'd enter. Turns out I'd been through 33 states, missing only 5 east of the Mississippi, and a lot of the other states I missed were states I still had never been in. Oh, well, next trip.

For the first time ever, I saw water in the Gila River, and wondered if there'd be any in the Salt River in Phoenix. For once, I thought, maybe the STORMWATCH!! banners on the L.A. stations were justified.

I reached Phoenix and saw the sign for Sky Harbor Airport, and thought about how I loved that name. Other than seeing water in the Salt River, though, I have nothing good to say about Phoenix. Trucks were driving in the left lane of the Interstate and a guy going well below the speed limit in the middle lane turned out to be, you guessed it, on the phone.

Not soon enough, I reached US 60 to Wickenburg, navigated through all the red lights on the highway, saw the traffic thin out and found a moment to look around. Broken clouds mottled the mountains to the northwest, towards Prescott, and more mountains became snow covered as I traveled farther north. Was that a harbinger, portent, omen, or boding of things to come? Yeah.

At a rest area on the banks of the Hassayampa River, an information board called it an upside down river, because most of its water flows in the aquifer. Well, maybe, but not today; there was quite a bit of water flowing, not deep, but wide and fast. In Wickenburg, I switched to US 93, aiming at I-40 east of Kingman.

I was having a few difficult moments because so much of this territory had been mine and Susan's, just before and after our marriage in Prescott. It surprised me a bit to be so affected after having been on the road so long, but then, so much of the road I'd traveled had never been with her and now memories were coming on fast and hard. As I passed through Wickiup, I remembered that a restaurant there had advertised Walla Walla burgers, and Susan used to joke that she wanted to make sure that the walla wallas had been shot with bow and arrow so as to not contaminate their meat. We never did stop to have one.

There was a lot of water in all the normally dry streambeds, and some beautiful scenery as sunshine alternated with cloud-shadow on the mountains that were sometimes white with snow and sometimes green with winter desert growth. I-40 reared its ugly head in the distance and I began to sweat the remaining miles available in my gas tank. I reached Kingman all right, though, and filled up at a station on its far side.

A gentleman from Idaho driving the same kind of Grand Marquis as mine bragged on his 27-mpg highway and told me I (at 22.9) had too heavy a foot. "Yeah," I thought, "Try driving as far as I have at 55 mph and you'd still be back there, somewhere." Told him off, eh?

Signs on US 93 warned of construction at Hoover Dam and that no trucks or busses would be allowed to cross the dam. I wondered if they might be building a bridge to take traffic off the dam, as a deterrent to terrorists, but didn't go all the way up there to find out. Instead, I turned off at Rte 68 to cross Golden Valley and saw snow on the peaks separating it and the Colorado River Valley beyond.

Once over the ridge, I could see lots of blue sky, the big bend of the Colorado, and a rock formation reminiscent of a hand flipping the bird. I got to the Flamingo Hilton, took a room on the 11th floor and watched a seaplane doing touch-and-go's on the river.

Laughlin was frustrating for me, in a way, because it's one of the few places I've been without a local access number for the Internet. I had been traveling with my laptop computer (and a cell phone) and gotten accustomed to checking email every night, sending messages to loved ones and, most important at this stage of the trip, checking road conditions in places I was going. In Laughlin I was helpless in this regard and had to rely on whatever news I could garner from the L.A. station the hotel piped in, if any, or from Las Vegas news. And we all know how visitor-unfriendly the local news shows can be, provincial in every regard.

The other reason Laughlin was frustrating was because Susan and I had gone there often together. We had made the trip from the Los Angeles area, usually leaving after traffic thinned around 7 PM on a Friday. We'd also gone from Prescott, leaving right after I finished work on Friday and intending to return on Sunday only to have the hotel make us an offer we couldn't refuse - $10 to stay on Sunday night. So we'd leave a wake-up call for 5 AM and we'd drive back to Prescott so I could walk in the office at 8 as though nothing had happened. I didn't want my assistant to know I'd been gambling, if she did, so would the entire Home Office.

And then, we'd spent our wedding night at the Flamingo.

After two days I left Laughlin. It was overcast; rain was in the forecast for everywhere west and I wasn't sure about how I was going to get home. First, I had to get to Los Angeles, actually Pasadena, to see my stepsons and their families. Imagine my surprise when I found snow falling on the west summit of the Colorado River canyon.

As I reached the California state line and drove down US 95 towards I-40 it was snowing on my left (east) while raining on my right. At this point, I knew it would be a long drive to Los Angeles, and that the spray of all the trucks that travel on it would obscure the Interstate. Fortunately, I had made lots of trips in the region and I knew a good alternative to I-40: I left US 95 to get on old Rte. 66. I drove through the town of Goffs, at the edge of the Mojave National

Preserve and under I-40; there, I could see that I was right about the truck traffic and visibility.

The National Trails Highway, as it's known, is the roadbed of old Rte. 66, and goes through a few small, once-prosperous towns, now fallen into decay as victims of Interstate bypass. There were a lot of dips in the stretch between Goffs and I-40, and I had to slow down in the event that there was running or standing water in them. I didn't recall ever having seen so much rain in the desert.

The road took me through the Fenner Valley; I don't know who Fenner was, and passed through Essex, CA, with a school and post office, but no active gas station or dwellings. As I reached Cadiz, the clouds began to break up and allow a little sunshine and, in the vicinity of Kelbaker Road I was able to see snow on the mountains up where the Interstate ran.

Nearby there were signs of some recent mining activity and lots of tailings. There is an amazing amount of mining in the Mojave, including a lot of lakebed scraping for minerals and salts, but I'm sure activities have been curtailed since the establishment of the Eastern Mojave Natural Preserve, a pet project of one of California's lady Senators. Fresh tailings surprised me.

Outside of Amboy I managed to pick up one of the desert radio stations and then lost reception just as they were about to announce road conditions at Cajon Pass, leading into the Los Angeles Basin. Since the pass was a lot higher than Amboy, I worried that it might have a good bit of snow, but I had to wait until I got there to find out.

In Amboy, a Café and Motel that had gone up just a few years before was now closed, marking the end of someone's hopes for a future in the desert. I thought about detouring over to 29 Palms and Yucca Valley and going into Los Angeles on I-10, but decided the mountains on that route were just as high as Cajon Pass and I wouldn't gain any-thing, especially time.

By now I was on dry roads and somewhere short of Ludlow I could see the Interstate traffic moving steadily. I may not have made much time on this route, but it was good to have had the freedom of the road and to remember some of the good times along it. Soon enough, I would be in all the traffic I could handle.

Ludlow was another victim of Interstate bypass, full of boarded up and falling down buildings. I expected to see water in the dry lake bed west of Newberry Springs, but there wasn't any and I again noted that I-40 was a dike road built to handle water accumulation in the lake. I made a smooth transition from I-40 to I-15 in Barstow and could now see some really dark clouds and bad weather ahead. I-15 had been improved to three lanes on the stretch between Barstow and Victorville and it was now a great highway, open and smooth. As the only surface route between Los Angeles and Las Vegas, it had always been congested.

In Victorville I saw the Mojave River flowing wide and fast, a stronger flow than I had ever seen in the 14 years I lived in Southern California. By now it was raining hard and visibility was limited. It was a Friday and the traffic going into L.A. was the lightest I'd seen, while the exodus in the other direction was pretty heavy.

At the crest of Cajon Pass traffic slowed to a crawl and I noticed that the road was cindered. Pretty soon the rain turned to snow and I slowly made my way down the mountain into the L.A. Basin. Halfway down, the snow turned back to rain, traffic began to speed up, but my windshield wipers weren't able to fully handle the volume of rain, and I got over to the right lane and eased down the pass at a reasonable speed. The rain continued to plague me all the way into Pasadena, and I heaved a tremendous sigh of relief when I reached my motel and settled in.

PART FOUR
NORTHBOUND AND UP

LAS VEGAS

It occurred to me how ironic it was that I had left Oregon to escape the winter rains, and here I was in the worst rains I had ever seen in Southern California. Oh, well.

I had also left Oregon to escape the memories of Susan's final days there. In Pasadena I was back in territory that had seen us meet, fall in love and begin our life together.

In 1996 one of my clients learned that I was single and invited me to the weekly open dance sponsored by his singles' organization. I delayed my appearance there, first to make a two-week trip through the Northwest and then to have minor surgery. Finally I showed up at the dance and he introduced me to several lady friends.

After I had chatted with them, he took me across the room to a table where several more ladies were sitting and, as I looked at them I thought, "Please let it be the blonde." Sure enough the blonde stood up and spoke in her delightful English accent. When my sponsor mentioned it I said, "Susan doesn't have an accent, we do." And the cash register rang up the points I made. KA-CHING!

I didn't leave her side that evening, and now that she is gone I regret any moment when I ever did.

I firmly believe we were destined to be soul mates. Though we disagreed about many trivial things we seemed to share values and desires about most of life's major challenges. Her sense of humor was dry and witty, she loved language and expression, and she never tired of exploring both places and ideas. We were good together.

When I got the opportunity to transfer to Prescott, AZ I proposed on bended knee, with a bouquet, at her place of work. For a moment I thought she might not accept, but it turned out that my surprise appearance was indeed a shock and I had caught her speechless. She accepted, my heart resumed beating and we went home to plan our married life.

Susan had been a nurse in England and in America she had begun a career in helping the developmentally disabled in finding and keeping gainful employment. She was unable to find work in Arizona, though, and we returned to the Los Angeles area six months later so that she could continue her career. During our travels we found that we were taken with the Carson Valley in Nevada and bought a house there, rented it out to tenants and looked forward to the time when we could segue into a calmer, gentler life style than that we enjoyed (?) in Southern California.

Regrettably, lung cancer struck her at about the time we were ready for the move. After her recuperation from surgery we made the transition to Nevada, only to discover that the thin air at mile high elevation caused Susan problems with breathing. As a result we moved down to sea level in Bandon. There we learned that the cancer had returned and it ultimately claimed her.

Susan loved the sea, as I suppose most Brits do. After all they grow up on an island. She used to remark that the south Oregon coast was very much like Wales, where she lived for a time, and it brought her great peace and happiness to just sit and watch the surf on the rocks or the waves lapping at the wide, empty beaches.

I had escaped Oregon's rains, but I will never escape my memories, and as far as most of them are concerned, I don't want to.

Seeing my stepsons, their wives/girlfriend, and my step-grandchildren was a delight. It always is, although the occasions are saddened terribly by Susan's absence. Beyond visiting with them, though, there was NOTHING I could do in Los Angeles in the horrible weather. Internet sites revealed that the tire chain law was in effect in places in California and Oregon between me and Bandon, and even though I carried chains, unused during the entire trip, I did what any self-respecting individual would do in the circumstances: I made reservations in Las Vegas.

There was water on the floor in the lobby of my motel, but none in the room where the continental breakfast was served. It was still raining hard, but I managed to get all my stuff into the car with a minimum of water accompanying it and got on my way to Vegas.

The mountains surrounding the Los Angeles area go as high as 10,000 feet and act as an effective barrier to water-bearing clouds coming in from the Pacific. That doesn't happen too often, storms usually pass to the north, but when it does, the basin gets drenched and only a little water makes it over to the desert.

I retraced my steps of a day ago along I-210 to I-15 and up Cajon Pass in a downpour that only got worse as I got closer to the mountains. It was foggy, raining hard and the few cars on the freeway were throwing up spray and STILL I encountered cars without their lights on. Well, whoever said safety was first in California?

The temperature was up in the 50s and I anticipated no snow on the pass this time. Sure enough, I encountered fog, but no snow, topped out at over 4,000 feet and drove into the high desert with sunshine in Hesperia and a big rainbow to my left. After crossing the Mojave River again, which was really a torrent, I saw the end of the rainbow touching the desert floor and apparently moving along with me as I drove on. I'd never been that close to a rainbow's end before and I thought, "No wonder you can't find the pot of gold, it won't stand still." And I also thought that I had always been chasing rainbows, my whole life long, and they always seemed to travel ahead of me, just out of my reach. The only rainbow I'd ever caught was Susan, and now she, too, was gone.

Again, there was a flow of water in the Mojave River in Barstow and that still impressed me. I couldn't remember the last time I'd taken I-15 to Vegas, but it occurred to me that I was now out of virgin road, that the way home from here would be on roads I'd driven before. I reflected on all my early trips to Vegas in the 80s, driving a broken-down Mercury and stopping at the Jenny Rose Café in Yermo, win, lose or draw. Once, I'd made it back to L.A. with the needle on Empty and my pockets empty, too.

On a straight stretch of highway, a water park, now called Rock-a-Hoda, looked like it had been spruced up in readiness for the summer season. It had opened, failed, opened again, failed again, and now it looked like new owners would give it a third try.

Out here, on cruise control at one mile an hour under the speed limit, I was getting passed like I was standing still. Southern California drivers, I think, vent their frustration with crawling freeways by opening it up in the desert. Yeah, I guess that's what I used to do. Vegas might move from there if I don't hurry.

I passed Afton Road, the turnoff to Afton Canyon, a beautiful stretch of the Mojave River through water-sculpted walls of sandstone. The river normally flows underground through the canyon, but I was willing to bet that there was plenty flowing through it above ground now.

Farther down the road was an exit sign for Zzyzx Road. Zzyzx is quite a story, named so as to be the last listing of place names in America. At one time a snake-oil salesman who called himself both a physician and a minister, but was neither, opened a health camp there, and broadcast over the radio for 30 years. He claimed the ability to heal, attracted both clients and their money and got closed down by the Feds for occupying government land without permission. The place is now used by California State University, and extension courses are offered through its Desert Studies Center.

The Devil's Playground is an area to the east of Baker that is basically a floodplain that marks the end of the Mojave River. I remembered that Bob and I almost got lost out there one winter after exploring Afton Canyon. We were trying to follow the Mojave Road from west to east with a guidebook that gave directions from east to west. I remember mumbling something about "intrepid explorers" as we sought a road to civilization. Needless to say, we made it.

Up on Mountain Pass, I saw the sign that marks the Kokoweef Mine, once described in an affidavit to the California Mining Board by a Mr. Carl Dorr in the 1930s. Seems there's supposed to be an underground river beneath the mountain with banks of black sand and gold nuggets. Explosives, placed there by Mr. Dorr to prevent others from entering the cave, conveniently sealed the natural cavern entrance, but he was sure he could find another where he'd seen a "shaft of light" from inside. Sure.

The thing is, there's substantial evidence of an underground river system in the Mojave, possibly drainage from the Great Basin. Remember all those rivers flowing in and none flowing out? Well, that water's got to go someplace, right? If you think you're lucky, you can look for the Kokoweef Mine and its river of gold.

There are other stories about lost mines in the desert, and whole books have been written about them. That there is gold in the Mojave is beyond question. The Yellow Aster mine in Randsberg has been working for a century. I've found gold in that vicinity at a mining claim owned by a prospecting club I belonged to in Southern California. There's nothing like a little color in your pan to lend credence to the legends and myths about gold out there. And there's nothing like a few days' hard work in the desert to cure you of searching for lost mines.

Death Valley Scotty, for whom Scotty's Castle is named although he didn't own it, used to talk about his gold mine and had many a believer. Scotty, a one time rider and roper with Buffalo Bill's Wild West Show befriended a Chicago insurance executive and regaled him with stories of the Old West. The executive built a castle at the north end of Death Valley and, shunning the limelight, he allowed Scotty's name to be attached to it. You can tour it anytime, courtesy of the National Park Service. Death Valley is within driving distance of Las Vegas and, in the wintertime at least, provides a refreshing side trip and relief from the gambling fever and bright lights. I didn't go on this trip.

Once down the last mountain in California, I noted that the dry lakebed of Ivanpah Lake, just shy of the Nevada line and bisected by I-15, was in fact, not dry. I'd never seen as much water in it.

Las Vegas hadn't changed much since my last visit, and I enjoyed driving the entire Strip from its desert origin to its downtown terminus, thanks to the fact that there was light traffic. I made a little money in the downtown casinos, and enjoyed the Fremont Street Light show.

I used the relatively new Frank Sinatra Drive to get from one Strip casino to another, via their back parking lots, and was disappointed to note that Caesar's Palace had changed its hiring policies and its waitresses were no longer the Queens of The Strip. The Bellagio water show was spectacular and I gave Mandalay Bay the Cocktail Waitress Best Costume Award. My, those girls were cheeky.

I enjoyed the distractions of Sin City and the gambling, but I found myself occasionally searching the casinos for Susan. She never wore a watch ("You Americans are so obsessed with the time.") and whenever we went to Vegas or

Laughlin it was impossible for us to arrange a time and place to meet. Casinos do NOT have clocks. We would agree not to leave any casino alone, though, and it was usually up to me to slowly scan the banks of nickel machines to find My Beloved. And every once in a while during this visit I spotted a blonde head and my heart skipped a beat. Then I came back to reality and moved on.

During my visit, I stayed out of town in Jean, NV, about 30 miles from Las Vegas, in a hotel that I had found when it was newly opened, back in 1988. The hotel has expanded during the years, but inflation hasn't quite caught up to it and its large rooms are still relatively inexpensive, $19.95 a night, as I recall. It provided a nightly refuge from the hustle of The Strip and served to cool the gambling fever that seems to take over my senses when I'm exposed to the, oh, so many ways to get rich. I once hit a royal flush for over a grand in its casino, but generally have been unlucky there; I'm sure they got the thousand back over the years.

BANDON

After three days, I left Vegas $160 to the good. I had paid for all my food and gas, and owed a hotel bill of about $60, so I considered it a win. I left the area under a cloudless sky, with good road conditions reported to the north. I was now on my final leg toward home, Northbound and Up, and intended to take three days to do it. I planned to stop overnight in Santa Nella and in Crescent City, which would allow me to arrive home before noon of the third day and get the house aired, heated and cleaned.

I had made lots of trips to Vegas in the late 80s and 90s, and I had returned sometimes flush, sometimes broke. I remember stopping at Whiskey Pete's on the border, trying to parlay a few bucks into a few more and failing. I made it home with naught but fumes in the tank that time. Another time I paid an exorbitant fee at a check cashing service on the Strip, walked into the old Aladdin and immediately hit a $100 jackpot on a quarter slot.

Vegas has changed somewhat with the times, though. It seems that the casinos felt a loss when the town tried to sell itself as a "family" vacation place. They then put in a lot of unattractive cost-control features, such as higher risk poker machines and made themselves less labor intensive by eliminating change people in favor of ticket printers and bill acceptors. What they've done is make the place less personable.

With Vegas behind me now, I recalled the TV news stories of the people who'd been caught in flooded areas of town trying to drive through swollen creek beds. My take on that is that they are rewarding stupidity when they interview those people and, instead of sparing their feelings, they should give them Darwin Awards. I once tried to cross a dry creek in the desert and bogged down in soft sand and I firmly believe I was really, truly stupid to do so. My rescue didn't involve TV crews or helicopters, just some wonderful people who happened to be passing by, and to whom I shall be eternally grateful. I would have been ashamed if I were interviewed.

Anyway, I was now traveling back south on I-15, off to my left the beautifully symmetrical Cima Dome rose gently on the horizon. Off to the right, I could see jagged peaks covered with snow and guessed the highest to be Telescope Peak, the dominant mountain in the Panamint Range overlooking Death Valley.

Descending from Halloran Summit, I could see water in both Soda Lake to the east of the highway, toward the Devil's Playground, and in the lake on the road to Death Valley from Baker, the one that generates such wonderful mirages. Yes, it really *was* water this time.

Back in Limon, CO I had bought lip balm for the arid climate of Denver and it was coming in handy now. I thought that, all the rain notwithstanding, nature was quickly taking the area back to a desert.

I passed Afton Canyon again, and thought, "Flow Gently, Sweet..." I could see water in the Mojave flowing into the canyon, and, again, it was something I'd never seen before. (NOTE: All this going on about the water in the desert was the result of some extremes in the weather pattern. Los Angeles recorded its third wettest winter ever by the time it was over, while the Northwest was experiencing a drought. After I returned to Bandon, I played golf in sunshine and 60 degree weather in January and February, almost unheard of in that region.) East of the Afton exit I encountered that same rippled road surface that apparently has had CalTrans baffled for years. I guess the land shifts frequently there and they just can't keep a level highway.

After passing the mountains outside of Yermo, where the old ghost town of Calico has been revived for tourists, and where green, ochre, red, brown and orange hues highlight the landscape, I encountered the California Agricultural Inspection Station and, since I wasn't carrying any fruit, they were closed.

At this point a KIA, a new one with the somewhat retro design being used by Chrysler and which I don't like, passed me. Retro fashions today are the very fashions my dad and his contemporaries wore/drove/bought and against which I rebelled as a young kid and teenager. I like them no better now than I did then. I still don't like pleated pants.

I reached Barstow and turned off on CA 58, saw turbulence in the Mojave River, snow on Mt. San Gorgonio and snow on the Tehachapis as well. I would cross the Tehachapis, the southern extension of the Sierra Nevada Range, over Tehachapi Pass, and I reflected that, except for Walker Pass out of Bakersfield, one had to go north to Reno and Donner Pass to cross the Sierra in the wintertime. Sometimes, Donner Pass and I-80 are closed, and I wondered if there was a comparable stretch of the Rockies that didn't have open passes in the winter.

Off to my right somewhere was Opal Mountain, to which Susan and I had taken the 4-wheel-drive truck in order to find the opals lying around on the ground. Well, we had to go see, didn't we? And if you had a 4WD truck, wouldn't you?

I could see the snow covered peaks of the Sierras peering over the nearer desert mountains and I was tempted to hang a right at Kramer Junction and follow US 395 up on one of the most gorgeously scenic drives I've ever made. But I feared that Donner Pass might be closed and drove on west.

After skipping 395 I passed through Boron, home of the largest borax mine in the country and was surprised to see its tailings to the north, I had always thought the mine was south of 58. The main drag through Boron is, of course,

Twenty Mule Team Road. With nothing else to look at in the Western Mojave, and with Edwards Air Force Base out of sight over the horizon, I looked straight ahead and saw clouds spilling over the Tehachapis and wondered about the weather in the Central Valley.

Outside of the city of Mojave, there's a dead airliner park, which, I've been told, is a holding place for airliners for sale. Seems to me there's an awful lot of old airplanes lying around. Mojave itself was a railhead, and the destination of the twenty mule teams that hauled borax out of Death Valley. Boraxo gave Ronnie Reagan a job on TV before his General Electric days. Remember "Death Valley Days" and Ron's predecessor, The Old Ranger?

I could see Telescope Peak behind me from the other side, and fields of wind turbines ahead, now being criticized for the bird deaths they are causing. Animal rights activists vs. environmentalists. Let's put 'em all in the ring and let 'em slug it out.

Before I knew it, I had bypassed Mojave on a brand new stretch of 58, new to me, anyway, and was on the upslope to Tehachapi Pass. The sign near the top read, "Welcome to Tehachapi, Land of Four Seasons," and I thought that was something to brag on in Southern California.

When I reached the summit, at 4,064 feet, I could see dense cloud ahead and figured that would be good for driving; I'd had intense sunshine all morning, and my eyes were feeling the glare. Train tracks passed through a lot of tunnels on their way down to the Tehachapi Loop, an engineering marvel that conquered a steep grade by looping the tracks in a circle, reducing the grade and often giving an engineer a chance to wave at his caboose as it passed under him. Really, back when they had cabooses.

There was thick fog at the bottom of the grade in the Central Valley and, while it was restful on my eyes, it did appear gloomy. I saw signs for the Weed Patch Highway and the Rosa Parks Highway, and in the middle of beautiful downtown Bakersfield I spotted a pickup truck with a bumper sticker, "VIVA Bush". I passed orange groves and nut orchards and soon after getting on I-5 saw a golden eagle on a fencepost.

I-5 is bordered by agriculture to the east as far as the eye can see, and by bare hills, green now from all the rain, to the west, an extremely uninteresting drive. My destination was Santa Nella and I left I-5 for CA 33 to loop through Mendota, Firebaugh and then Los Banos, in an effort to relieve the monotony, and drive at least a short stretch of virgin road. It was another extremely uninteresting drive; I should have stayed on the Interstate.

In Santa Nella, a guy in a pickup ran the 4-way stop and almost creamed me; I was recording at the time and dropped the tape recorder, which faithfully got all my language and the sound of my horn blowing angrily, but I had to laugh as I could see the guy's wife giving him hell.

Overnight in Santa Nella was unremarkable.

When I left in the morning, after sleeping in until 6:30, I had mixed feelings about sticking to the original plan and stopping in Crescent City. On the one hand, it would be cold and damp in Bandon if I drove straight through and I'd have to get the house warm and go shopping and lots of etcs. On the other hand, I'd be HOME.

Halfway to Oakland I decided to call my neighbor Cindy, whose husband was doing some work for me in the house and ask her to turn up the heat and open the kitchen window. She heartily agreed to do so, and I now made Bandon my day's destination.

Closer to Oakland the traffic started to thicken but it kept moving, thinned and I made it through town, onto the Richmond Bridge and northbound on US 101, the last highway I would need to use to get home. I got past the bottlenecks of Petaluma and Santa Rosa, which weren't bottlenecks at all that day, and felt that I could coast home.

Now the memories returned of the many trips Susan and I had taken to and from Los Angeles for her treatment. We were trapped within the confines of the health care system we had when she was diagnosed, and it took us nearly a year to get care transferred to Oregon. In the meantime we made the best of it by enjoying the scenic part of the trip, from the Bay Area northwards.

That part of US 101 has its unique features:

- Healdsburg Veterans Memorial Beach, miles from the ocean.

- Alexander Valley, which is coming on as a wine grape-growing region to rival Sonoma and Napa.

- Ukiah, "Pretty Valley" in the language of whatever Injuns we displaced from the area and who are now getting their revenge many times over through local casinos.

- Ridgewood Summit, between Ukiah and Willets, a normally treacherous climb with narrow lanes, made doubly so by construction.

- Willets, always a foggy place when I pass through it.

- Leggett, which has a drive-through tree and is the northern terminus of CA 1, the coast road.

- Garberville, south of which the highway narrows to fit between giant redwoods and is the home of yet another Benbow Inn.

- The Avenue of the Giants, which parallels 101 for a number of miles, but affords much closer looks at the giant redwoods.

- 40 miles south of Eureka is a sign for the Humboldt Area Pagan Network, whatever that is.

- The large lumber mill at Scotia was working but certainly not to the level it must have been in its heyday.

- Victorian Ferndale is a wonderful town to visit, if you like old stuff. Or if, like Susan, you just want to walk into a store and ask for an antimacassar and discover that they know what you're talking about.

- Finally, just south of Eureka, a glimpse of the Pacific Ocean. Sea to shining sea, indeed. And, back again.

I was very proud of myself for getting through Eureka in 7 minutes, via some skilful lane changing and minor lawbreaking. Once on the other side, I realized I was making wonderful time, and would be in Bandon by 6 P.M. I stopped at the Trinidad rest stop and reflected that it was the prettiest rest stop I'd ever been in, a very tranquil place. Up toward Orick I passed the little red schoolhouse where there are usually elk, but alas, there were none this day. Orick has the world's largest Bureau of Land Management building. At least, I think so.

In Klamath, CA I saw my first sign for smoked salmon, then went over the dreaded mountain that separates it from Crescent City. The forest on that leg is truly primeval. At Smith River, named for Jedediah, and tagged as the Easter Lilly Capital of the World, I could see the St. George's Reef Lighthouse, well out to sea, and the All Star Liquor Store, where I stopped to get California Lottery tickets. Finally in Oregon, I gassed up in Brookings; felt that it was nice to be in a place where I couldn't pump my own gas and also to be legal with a concealed weapon again.

Near Gold Beach, I passed the 12,000-mile mark on the journey, and then circled Humbug Mountain to reach

Port Orford. I pulled into my own driveway at 6 P.M. on the dot, and entered the house to find it warm. There was a plate of food on the kitchen counter for me together with several pieces of cake, and a bowl of chicken soup in the refrigerator, all welcome home presents from my neighbors. And it brings tears to my eyes to write about that.

Dorothy was right.

There IS no place like home.

I had traversed the nation, out across the north half and back across the south. I had stayed in hotels and motels and been a guest and a guest, again. I had tried to leave my grief behind me but it managed to catch up with me each time I was alone. Now I was home again, through with escaping, face to face with the harsh reality of living alone and having to come to grips with life. I had guessed that travel would "cure" me of loneliness and grief, but it hadn't and now I had to guess again.

There is a healing process that will take place no matter where I live, and it will eventually erase the horror of Susan's final days. I will heal, and remember her and the good times we had. I will heal. Slowly.

EPILOGUE

I put the finishing touches to this book over a year after completing the trip. In that year, I found romance, left Bandon for a while, lost romance and returned. It was far too soon for me to get involved with another woman. My grief has continued to be a significant, but manageable part of my life.

In the summer of 2005, my routine physical led to a diagnosis of Chronic Lymphocytic Leukemia, a relatively slow acting cancer of the blood, and the same oncologist who treated Susan is now treating me.

I went back to Corpus Christi and, instead of buying, decided to rent a condo there for coming winters. I'll play a lot of golf, both in Texas and here in Bandon.

I tried out for, and won, a part in our local Readers' Theater presentation of some old radio shows. I joined the local writers' group and who knows what'll come from me next.

I've often said that I have no regrets about decisions I've made in life, some of them led to wonders, some to tragedies. But I do regret that Susan and I never stopped for a Walla Walla burger. It would have been one more wonderful thing to remember.

Made in the USA
Monee, IL
07 July 2026

56551277R00092